D0736109

Book BLITZ

Getting Your
Book In The News

Book BLITZ

Getting Your
Book in the News

60 Steps to a
Best Seller

by

Barbara Gaughen
and
Ernest Weckbaugh

Burbank, Hollywood and Santa Barbara, California

Photos on cover and biography pages by Madeleine's Photography (Barbara Gaughen) and Richard Williams Photography and Antonios Zamouzakis Photography (Ernest Weckbaugh)

10   9   8   7   6   5   4   3   2

ISBN 1-881474-02-X
Library of Congress Catalog Card Number 93-73030

Best-Seller Books™
Burbank, Hollywood, Santa Barbara

Best-Seller Books • 1718 Rogers Place, Suite 1A, Burbank, CA 91504
226 East Canon Perdido, Suite B1, Santa Barbara, CA 93101

Book and cover design by Ernest Weckbaugh, Casa Graphics, Inc.
Manufactured in the United States of America by Delta Lithograph Co.

Dedicated to
authors everywhere...
may your book be a
runaway best seller!

A special dedication to
Patty, Barbie and Dave

Acknowledgments . . .

Book BLITZ has been nourished from many sources—family, friends, co-workers, business associates and many talented authors. This book would not now be in your hands without them.

When the first draft was finished, it was sent out to authors, publicists and media friends, and their comments were solicited. These experienced contributors sent back pages covered with notes. They made this book far more than we thought possible.

Principal editorial help came from Patty Weckbaugh, Sinara Stull O'Donnell and Andrea Daniel. Our excellent peer reviewers were Bill Cannon, Renee Cooper, Vega Dean, Ted Gardner, Francis Halpern, Frederic Hudson, Bruce Katz, John Lewis, Pam MacLain, Cork Millner, Dan Poynter, John Spaulding, Joyce Wycoff and Karyn Young.

Our case study article resources, writers or interviewees were Caroline Arnold, Penny Ayeroff, Dick Beals, Eve Bunting, Gwen Carden, Doris Cross, Emily Dee, Clarrissa Pinkola Estes, David Evans, Virginia Fleming, Elisabeth Handler, Joni Hilton, Tony Johnston, Ruth Klein, Jane Kurtz, Lael Littke, Barry Martin, Marcus Meleton, Marlys Milhiser, Tom Miller, Sinara Stull O'Donnell, Don Parker, Dan Poynter, Tom and Marilyn Ross, Elisabeth Sifton, Aaron Silverman, Tena Spears, Martha Tolles, Dottie Walters and Irwin Zucker. The inspiration for the title *BLITZ* was provided by Doran William Cannon.

To these people we give our special thanks.

Now we wish to acknowledge you, the reader, for *your* future contributions to *Book BLITZ*. It would be of great value to us and to the future revisions of this book if you would share your book promotion experiences.

Mail or fax to: Best-Seller Books, 226 E. Canon Perdido, Suite B1, Santa Barbara, CA 93101
Fax: (805) 965-6522

Foreword . . .

Dan Poynter

Whether you are self-published or have turned your manuscript over to a publisher, the author always has to do the book promotion. Most authors find out too late that publishers do not promote books. "If it is to be, it's up to me." You need guidance and encouragement—***Book BLITZ* will be your coach.**

Plan your product. Find a need and fill it. Target your audience before you write your book. Who are your readers and what do they want? How can you help them by delivering the most value while taking the least amount of their time? You need something to lean on and ***Book BLITZ* will be your escort.**

You can always promote an old book, but it is better to plan your promotion before you write your next book. Read this book, then draft your marketing plan. You need a map and ***Book BLITZ* will be your guide.**

Writing your book is the easy part—the tip of the iceberg. The real work begins when you switch hats to expend time and money on promoting your book. As you enter this new territory, ***Book BLITZ* will be your beacon.**

Book promotion takes time. Book reviews take three months to three years to appear because magazines and even daily newspapers have long lead times. The most common mistake is to send out books for review, news releases on your book or a direct-mail offer and then sit back and wait for the results. The secret of savvy book promotion is to keep up the pressure: keep sending out the packets and keep making those phone calls. You need a constant reference and ***Book BLITZ* will be your mentor.**

Barbara Gaughen and Ernie Weckbaugh have made your new venture easy by dividing the trip into 60 steps. Start now by taking that first step. ***Book BLITZ* will be your secret weapon.**

Dan Poynter
The Self-Publishing Manual

PREFACE
by Barbara Gaughen

Dr. Edward Crowther was worried about his book when he called me. It had been published in hardback by a small, independent publisher and then picked up for publication in paperback. Dr. Crowther believed the topic *(Intimacy: Strategies for Successful Relationships)* was hot and the time was right...but something was obviously wrong because it wasn't selling. After I looked at his book, I agreed with him and we decided to work together to promote it.

In Chase's *Directory of Events,* I discovered "Kiss Your Mate" day was coming up soon. We sent a press release to the media suggesting that they interview Dr. Crowther about ideas for increasing intimacy. (The stamp we used showed a couple hugging.) Within two weeks, Dr. Crowther was

called by Phil Donohue's people and almost immediately wound up on the show as an expert working with three dysfunctional couples.

Throughout the show, Donohue carried Dr. Crowther's book with the title showing at all times. The book quickly sold off the shelves and continues to sell well, periodically boosted by the repeat of that popular Donohue segment.

Dr. John Lewis is a retired surgeon who wrote the book *So Your Doctor Recommended Surgery,* published by a major publisher. Dr. Lewis called me because his book wasn't selling. We targeted insurance company newsletters and sent them an article excerpted from the book. One of the newsletters was spotted by the *National Enquirer* which ran an article about Dr. Lewis' Book. This led to additional articles in health magazines. Sales flourished and the book was released in paperback.

Every day I get calls from authors with sad book stories. They don't understand why their book isn't selling. Sometimes they can't even find it on the shelf in book stores. Generally, they make the classic mistake of most new authors. They assume the publisher will promote their book. The publishing industry is an interesting phenomenon and the subject of endless, sometimes heated, discussions between authors, publishers, agents and editors. But if there is a rule of thumb to go by, it's this: when it comes to promotion, you are far safer assuming the publisher *won't* do it than assuming he will.

Unless you happen to be one of the top, best-selling authors, promotional efforts of your book will be minimal. Which means, if you want your book to sell, it's your job to promote it. The time to start is now! Even if you haven't finished writing your book, it's not too early to think about the marketing. Who's the target market? Who might provide recommendations for the book jacket? Which magazines would be most likely to review it? What publications would be interested in article excerpts?

Based on my years of successful book marketing and researching of the nation's best sellers, I am convinced that more books are *marketing* failures than *writing* failures. Every author puts a lot of hard work and effort into writing a book. Why let it fail for lack of the proper promotion? "Out of print" is an ugly phrase, especially when there are people out there who need the information in your book or would enjoy reading the story your book tells.

The book promotion techniques you will learn in the following chapters have been effective in helping other authors greatly increase their book sales. It's important to remember that each author and each book is different. What works for one person may not be right for you. You are the expert on your book. Make sure that any promotional efforts you undertake fit who you are and your target market. We can learn from the thoughts and experiences of others, but only to the extent that they help us discover our own directions. If this book is to have any value for you, you need to take the ideas here and adapt them to you own circumstances.

For most authors, a book is a piece of themselves, an act of creation not unlike that of having a child. But for the work to thrive it has to be read, and to be read, people have to know about it. Not spending the time and effort to promote a book would be like not providing an infant with food and shelter.

The time and effort you've put into writing your book says you believe in the inherent value of its message. There are people who need to hear what you have to say. Book promotion isn't about convincing people to buy your book. It's about knowing where to find the people who are waiting for it. I hope the following ideas and promotional techniques help your book meet with the success it truly deserves.

Q. **What is a best seller?**

A. You'll know you're a best seller when you find your book on a "Best Seller List" compiled by the . . .

New York Times
Publishers Weekly
Chicago Tribune
San Francisco Chronicle

Q. **How do you make these best seller lists?**

A. It begins with you and your diligence with *Book BLITZ* . . . from your Checklist to the "Best Seller List," it can happen to you!

Read on.

TABLE OF CONTENTS

Congratulations! Your book is published! Celebrate!

After the book is published

INTRODUCTION
by Ernest Weckbaugh

There is a story attributed to the great filmmaker Cecile B. DeMille. Once, while fishing, he happened to observe a beetle-like naiad crawl from the water's edge to the muddy bank and onto a rock. There in the sun it slowly "died." Its shell cracked open and a thick fluid oozed out. What DeMille was actually watching in fascination was the final act of metamorphosis—the shedding of its outer shell from which emerged a delicate dragonfly. With its iridescent green body and four lacy wings, the tiny naiad, or nymph, had evolved into a mature adult and would soon be able to fly.

In a moment of reflection, DeMille must have pondered...*If the Creator allowed this lowly creature to experience such a liberating change—from lake-bottom mud to the vast expanse of the sky—what does that tell us about the human potential?*

This metaphor also typifies the author who must

suddenly evolve into the publicist. Promoting one's self and book through personal appearances, book tours, news releases and interviews must seem totally contrary to anyone who has led the solitary life of putting words on paper.

Nevertheless, there comes a time when we need to take wing and lift our precious creation upward and make it visible for all to see. For the newly-published book there is simply no one else who will do it.

"But doesn't the publisher do that?" every new author asks. Those who really believe that would probably feel optimistic about landing on something soft after jumping without a parachute from thousands of feet.

"The publisher takes care of all sales and publicity efforts" is a very common but, unfortunately, false assumption. The balance of this book will explain what we, as writers, can and must do about book promotion, and how. Those who have managed to sustain a writing career understand this obligation and participate willingly in the publicity phase of their book's production. They know the job isn't over until someone takes care of this vital necessity. They know that "someone" is the author. Happily, most of them find the experience enjoyable.

The experience quoted on pages 5 and 170, by Marlys Milhiser, speaks of her walking into a new bookstore in a distant city and finding her book there. There could only be one thing more thrilling to an author: *NOT* finding it there because it was sold out. Among the sweetest words an author can hear are when a proprietor says, "We just can't seem to keep your book on the shelf."

That situation has everything to do with you, and little to do with your publisher. Only those authors who find themselves consistently on the best-seller list rate the full support of a major publisher. One has to wonder what kind of effort on the part of these well-known authors was required over the years to finally get them on the publisher's "A" list.

Inventories of publishers the world over are stocked with unsold books. Why? Because the most important part of the job was left undone—the author failed to take the responsibility for developing an awareness of, or a constituency for his or her product.

Yes, your book *is* a product, according to Harvey MacKay, the best-selling author of *Swim With The Sharks Without Being Eaten Alive* (William Morrow and Company, Inc.) You may think your book has a timeless message or may be a great, epic piece of art. Unless it's sold with the same kind of shrewd and shameless intensity as a new automobile or a new line of perfume, no one will ever know, or care.

We're here to make you, the author, aware of both your responsibilities and your privileges. We're here to show the steps involved as clearly and as simply as possible. We're here to help you feel the joy of showing off your "baby" to an awaiting world. We're here to make *you* the best seller of your book in the eyes of your publisher, *especially* if that publisher is yourself.

Important note: All of the above and the rest of the book may seem a bit overwhelming to you. If you didn't feel that way you would be the rare exception, but anything is possible one simple step at a time. You need to realize that promoting your own book will:

- Require a time commitment.
- Interrupt your otherwise quiet lifestyle.
- Call on all of your social and performance skills, or ones you may yet need to develop.

However, the link between writing and making contact with your readers is essential. As you read on, ask yourself if you really have a choice.

"I walked into a brand new bookstore in Chicago unannounced and found my book there. I passed a B. Dalton in a Las Vegas mall and saw copies I'd previously signed displayed face out at the front of the store. I had the thrill of meeting fans, both old and potential. I did a talk and reading in Albuquerque on a Saturday night and realized that people who had simply wandered in to browse had stopped to listen. Many of them stayed to ask questions, some even bought books."

Author Marlys Milhiser

60

Steps

to

"Instant"

Success

Weeks before and after book is printed	20	16	12	9	8	7	6	5	4	3	2	1	0	1	2	3	4	5	6	*Indefinitely* →
1 Refocus on your book's target audience	●																			
2 Develop a strategic plan		●																		
3 Develop list of publications/reviewers interested in your book			●																	
4 Send bound galleys and query letters to selected editors				●																
5 Prepare a media release that reporters will read and publish					●	●	●	●	●	●	●	●	●	●	●	●	●	●	●	●
6 Send out the media release(s) as needed for newsworthy items					●	●	●	●	●	●	●	●	●	●	●	●	●	●	●	●
7 Develop a brochure or flyer			●	●																
8 Send your brochures/flyers with a "bounce-back" to reviewers				●	●															
9 Participate in "Books for Review"				●																
10 Compile a list of targeted organizations				●	●															

11 Phone organizations to discuss offer to members

12 Send out brochure/flyer to direct mail audience

13 Prepare a press kit

14 Phone major TV shows

15 Send press kits to interested TV shows

16 Prepare pre-publication announcement ads

17 Send announcement to key buyers

18 Phone call follow-up to media

19 Review (and adjust) your strategic plan

20 Run pre-publication ads

Weeks before and after book is printed	20	16	12	9	8	7	6	5	4	3	2	1	0	1	2	3	4	5	6	Indefinitely →
21 Mail pre-publication offer to targeted organization/audience							●	●												
22 Plan non-traditional promotional programs						●	●	●	●											
23 Contact larger book wholesalers/distributors						●	●	●												
24 Follow-up larger wholesalers with mailing								●	●											
25 Mail brochures/flyers to smaller wholesalers								●	●											
26 Mail brochures/flyers to major bookstore chains								●												
27 Phone follow-up to bookstore chains															●	●	●			
28 Conduct mailing to independent bookstores																●	●			
29 Send targeted mailing to specialized bookstores																●	●			
30 Participate in co-op bookstore mailings															●	●	●			

31 Advertise or list book in special magazine editions

32 Participate in book fairs and trade shows

33 Register with the American Bookseller Association

34 Contact library distributors and wholesalers

35 Contact magazines about periodical rights for excerpts

36 Contact magazines about condensation rights

37 Contact book clubs

38 Contact foreign book publishers

39 Brainstorm non-traditional markets

40 Research and develop list of specialty book stores

Weeks before and after book is printed	20	16	12	9	8	7	6	5	4	3	2	1	0	1	2	3	4	5	6	*Indefinitely* →
41 Mail brochures/flyers to targeted specialty book stores										●	●	●								
42 Test other stores/markets with phone survey										●	●									
43 Mail to catalog houses										●										
44 Pursue premium offers										●	●	●	●	●	●					
45 Pursue bookshelves										●	●									
46 Your book is published													○							
47 Send out advance review copies to major media														●	●					
48 Photograph book cover for press kits/post cards														●						
49 Plan author tour, book signings, etc.														●	●	●	●	●	●	
50 Target mailings to library/book trade publications														●	●					

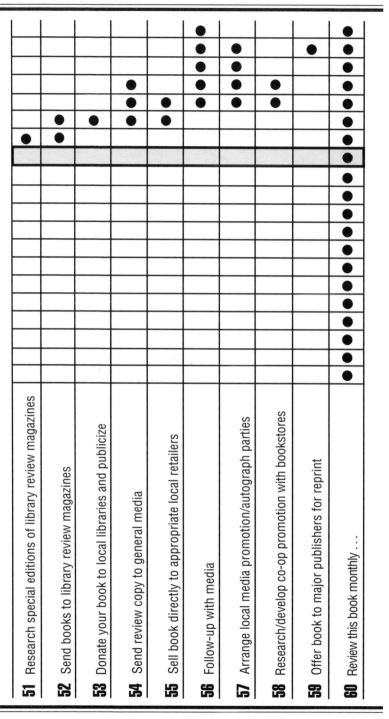

51 Research special editions of library review magazines

52 Send books to library review magazines

53 Donate your book to local libraries and publicize

54 Send review copy to general media

55 Sell book directly to appropriate local retailers

56 Follow-up with media

57 Arrange local media promotion/autograph parties

58 Research/develop co-op promotion with bookstores

59 Offer book to major publishers for reprint

60 Review this book monthly . . .

CHAPTER ONE

You're *the Best Seller of Your Best Seller*

—Chapter One—
This is a book full of good news! **You** *are in*
charge here. **You** *can make things happen.*
You *are the one who can cause your book*
to be a Best Seller. Here's how. . .

Introducing
THE SIXTY STEPS

Are you looking for a Best Seller? Look no more.
It's *you!*

If you've bought a good book lately, chances are a
friend told you about it or you heard of it through some
form of publicity, which is probably how your friend
heard about it. It could have been either a radio or TV
interview with the author, a book review in the newspaper or perhaps a book club write-up. Even if you bought
it because it caught your eye on the book store shelf, it's
important to realize that all of these things happen
because of the book's promotion.

Best sellers are made, not born. Authors who intend
to have their book reach the broadest possible audience
need to shift gears from their life of quiet seclusion in
front of their word processors to the role of book market-
ers and salespeople. These authors should know that
their agent doesn't do it for them, their editors can't do it
and their publishers won't do enough of it.

So, if you want a Best Seller, it has to be *you*. Whether you are self-published or have a major publisher, you are responsible for the promotion of your book. To help you know what to do and exactly when to do it, the following pages contain a step-by-step guide to successful book promotion. These steps are loaded with insider tips and insights from book promotion professionals, people who have spent entire careers learning the specific book promotion techniques passed along to you in the following chapters. We will also give you dozens of stories from our experience with authors who have lifted their book sales to new heights by following these simple steps.

In 1988, the Wall Street Journal reported that even best-selling authors were hiring their own publicists to help push their books because publishers weren't willing to put enough time, effort and money behind them.

If big-time writers need help, what about the little guy? What chance do first-time authors have to get the kind of attention essential to move their books off the shelf and into the hands of eager readers? Not much...unless they know what the professionals know and do what the professionals do.

And you can. The following 60 steps are your guidelines...they give you the information you need to be the best seller of your Best Seller.

ME, A SALESPERSON?

Too often writers imagine that their problems are over once they get that long-sought contract in their hands. Most writers would rather not deal with the business of selling books. But, unless you're Danielle Steele or Tom Clancy, your book publisher probably isn't going to put much time or effort into promoting your book. They simply don't have the vested interest you do in your book. However, as soon as a book starts to do well, as in the case of Rush Limbaugh's *The Way Things Ought To Be*, publishers are quick to up the ante, throwing more of their money behind the publicity effort. His book has now beaten all publishing sales records. Limbaugh, of course, has his own talk shows on radio and television. It's safe to assume he put forth a great publicity effort on his own from the very beginning. Unless that kind of push is made by you, the individual author, you are likely to see disheartening gaps on the book store shelves where your book ought to be, your book ignored by the reviewers, and minuscule, or even non-existent, royalty checks.

The publisher's lack of promotional efforts probably doesn't make sense to you. The average investment in a new book ranges from $20,000 to $50,000. Why don't they make every effort to protect that investment? It's probably because they're operating on the 80/20 principle. Around the beginning of the 20th Century, an Italian economist/sociologist by the name of Vilfredo Pareto conceived this theory after concluding that, at any given time in history, roughly eighty percent of the nation's goods and services were produced by only about twenty percent of Italy's population.

Today, we've found that the 80/20 rule applies to many situations where eighty percent of the results are created by twenty percent of the producers. Book publishing profits follow this rule: The "blockbuster" books carry the rest of the publisher's inventory. Too often, the non-blockbusters languish in the warehouse waiting to be remaindered and labeled with the ugliest of all phrases: "Out of print." Of course, the publisher hopes one or more of these warehouse sleepers will take off and prove to be a fiscal phenomenon, but they're not willing to bet much time, money or effort on it.

If you expect to be called by newspaper, radio, or TV folks eager to interview you about your book...If you've

picked out a new wardrobe for a whirlwind book tour...
Even if you just want to see your book reviewed in the
Sunday supplement of your local paper, *YOU HAVE TO
MAKE IT HAPPEN!*

ME, IN THE MEDIA?

Barbara Gaughen recently telephoned the Joan
Rivers Show in order to schedule a book author for an
upcoming show. The producer, Mariann Sobol, told her
about one of her pet irritations with telephone pitches.

"I hate it when agents call me and pitch a story
(interview) idea when neither they nor their clients have
even bothered to watch the show. From what they say to
me, they obviously don't know the show's format, and
yet they proceed to pitch an inappropriate idea at great
length ... with gusto!"

In the following chapters, we will show you how to
target your promotional efforts so you're offering producers what they want. But that means meetings and
interviews! The number one adult fear is speaking in
front of people, a camera, or a microphone. Most writers
didn't pick the writing game because of their love for
public speaking. You can't, however, stay hidden in the
closet and expect your book to sell itself.

The obligation to meet the public, either one-on-one,
in front of hundreds or facing a TV camera with an
audience of millions is an essential part of promotion.
There is no putting it off or getting around it. The
author promotes his or her current book in order to get
the chance to write the next one. The sooner you get
used to an audience and start listening to their helpful
evaluations to improve your presentation, the easier all
of this will become.

One author had parties in his home during the time
he was finishing his book, in order to stage mock interviews or try out speeches in front of his friends. He'd set

up chairs in his front room, have microphones and a stage-like setting at one end of the room and, after everyone had eaten the buffet dinner, he was on. He asked for suggestions for improvements after he concluded and spent an hour taking notes. He was careful to invite people who were used to evaluating speakers, people who were good speakers themselves.

Waiting to get this kind of practice until the last minute when the panic sets in, is like the heart attack victim who listens carefully to the doctor's advice *after* he's in the hospital. He's hearing the same things he heard years before, only now he's paying attention. The best time to start building your public confidence is when you start your book, not after you finish it. Being at ease in front of the public takes time and practice and deserves the same commitment and attention to detail as you bring to your writing efforts.

Confidence can be developed over time at low cost with minimal intimidation in friendly self-help organizations such as Toastmasters International, or you can pay a professional media trainer a professional price to give you an intensive, overnight crash course. However, since you know public appearances *will* be part of your future plans, you might consider the slower, more relaxed, low-impact style of training. It's much easier on your budget and your nerves.

Interviews and public appearances are going to be part of your professional life as a writer, the same as any other celebrity. It's in your best interest to be available, friendly and informative. Public figures in show business, sports and politics know that their very survival can depend on their press relations. An understanding of all of this and what is expected of you can help you become more effective at selling your book. In the same way a writer needs to know what a publisher wants, he or she also needs to be keenly aware of what the public and the media want. The better prepared you are, the better performer you will be.

CASE STUDY: *Ready or Not!*

Even well-published authors suffer from poor publicity, or sometimes no publicity. Lael Littke, author of approximately 30 books for young people, was asked by a book store manager to autograph books at his store when he learned she was to be in his city. She agreed to do it. When she arrived, she found that no preparation had been done in anticipation of her visit. No ad had been placed in the local newspaper announcing her appearance. No fliers had been mailed to the store's regular customers. There were no signs displayed in the mall around the store. No host directed people to her as they entered the store. No one explained who she was or why she was there. There was a table with stacks of her books on it and a chair for her to sit on, but that was all.

A number of people did stop by, curious as to why she was sitting there. She engaged them in conversation and many of them, expressing pleasure at meeting her, bought books. But the experience was not quite what she'd expected.

"It would have made a difference if there'd even been a sign saying who I was and what I was doing there," she said. "It would have helped if the clerks had been primed to direct people my way. If I'd known ahead of time that there was to be no publicity, I could have done my own promotion, mailing flyers to my friends in the city and perhaps asking one of them to be my 'greeter' at the store."

What else could have been done? An author

might bring her own posters with pictures and listings of her books and awards. She might convince the bookstore owner to hand out one-dollar discount coupons to encourage people to buy the author's books.

"Another store where I signed," Littke said, "had me give a short speech in a nearby room while I was there. The manager encouraged people to come hear me and bring their children. They could find out who I was and they could ask questions about my books. That worked very well."

Presumably the reason a manager invites an author to sign is to attract people into the store so they will buy books. It benefits the store as well as the author when the event is well publicized. The author is well advised to discuss the publicity with the store manager when she agrees to do a signing. There should be an understanding as to what the manager will do and what the author herself will bring.

Sometimes even books that receive numerous honors may not sell well. For instance, one of Littke's recent books won high praise from such review magazines as *Publisher's Weekly* and *Horn Book* as well as being a Junior Literary Guild selection and winning the 1991 "Notable Book Award" from the Southern California Council on Literature for Children and Young People. Yet it has not sold well.

Why? Perhaps the publisher's sales representatives did not push it. Perhaps its gentle jacket illustration was not sensational enough to capture interest. Perhaps it simply got lost in the avalanche of new children's books. Awards, all by themselves, just aren't enough to bring a book to the public's attention and make people want to buy it.

There's an old saying that states: *Build a better mousetrap and the world will beat a path to your door.* Thousands of failed inventors and starving authors know how wrong that statement is. Just writing a quality book won't move the world to action. You need to be sure that everyone knows about it.

TIPS: On titling and typos

It's important to note here that creating a high-quality book is essential for an author to succeed at publicizing it. If the book falls short in production values, how it looks to the consumer, no amount of "hype" is going to help it.

It's a lot easier and more satisfying to stand before your public with pride than with apology. Here are two areas of your writing project that make all the difference whether your promotional effort will pay off or not.

A stimulating title and error-free typesetting can play a big part in the book's saleability. Distributors will often avoid self-publishers, knowing that many of them aren't too careful about quality. Keep your title options open as long as possible for that last-minute inspiration.

TITLING:

Rule One—Keep it simple. Eve Bunting, the author of 150 children and young adult books, found this rule to be true with her title *If I Asked You, Would You Stay?* It was praised by those who read it, but no one could ever remember the title.

Another one of her books with a long title proved to be the exception. *Karen Keppel White Is the World's Best Kisser* sold well because the youthful buzz words *World's Best Kisser* were irresistible to young readers.

Rule Two—Put a "hook" in it. When your book sits on a shelf awaiting the buyer, you want it to stand out from the rest. You need a title that will create an impulse to reach out, pick it up and buy it.

Rule Three—Try to make the *first* word in the title indicate the subject. Otherwise, the computer in the library or bookstore that searches for the subject, and the titles by first word only, could completely miss your book. Since nearly everyone looks for a book by its subject first, you're also smart to put the key word — the subject — up front. The average person looking through a card catalog section of a library will give up in a minute if your title can't be found.

Rule Four—Avoid words like *Guide, How To, Complete, New, Everything,* or *Illustrated.* Library and bookstore computers contain dozens of columns, with hundreds of titles *ALL* beginning with *The Illustrated...,* or *The Complete...,* etc. Who's going to take time to find yours? Put the *How to* and *Complete* in your subtitle.

Rule Five—Remember library microfiche machines allow for only 30 characters. With a short title and sub-title, each letter and space between words must give the whole meaning in 30 spaces. Make every word count.

Rule Six—A title can suggest *everything* about the subject. Tony Robbins' *Awaken The Giant Within* has self-improvement written all over it. A book with a title like *Thin Thighs In Thirty Days,* by Wendy Sehling, leaves no doubt that it's about exercise. Alliteration, as in the repetition of "th" three times, is also very popular in titling because it aids the memory. Dr. Seuss' *Horton Hatches a Who* quickly comes to mind. Sales can happen when your book title comes easily to everyone's memory.

Martha Tolles, an author of eight books with total sales of over two million, found that alliteration and buzz words work for her. She polled a number of children (her potential readers) and they chose *Sarah's Secret* over *Motel Family* as the title for her new book.

Rule Seven—A title can also be successful if it explains *nothing* about the subject. Richard Nelson Bowles book entitled *What Color Is Your Parachute* works because it's unusual, colorful and teases the book buyer into picking up the book after saying to himself, *"What?"* But a book with a title like that needs a lot of promotion, or the public won't recall what it's about.

Rule Eight—Books with titles that name new concepts also need more than a normal amount of publicity. *Theory Z,* by William Ouchi, introduced the revolutionary idea of consensus decision-making, a style of management practiced by the Japanese. Once the public became aware of the book, its title was quickly accepted as a new word in our language. *I'm Okay, You're Okay* is a "concept book" by Thomas A. Harris. It's about Transactional Analysis, and it helped to package a new movement in psychology.

Rule Nine—Title words whose very sound suggests violent action like *sting* or *kill* promise excitement. There's a buzzing quality about them. Abstract words like *beyond, rich, easy* or *quick* stir imagination, curiosity and interest in luxury or convenience.

Slang or trendy words like *disco* or *groovy* fall out of fashion quickly and tend to date a book. Sinister words like *murder, foul play* or *deadly* have been in style for sensational titles since Eighteenth-Century England, and probably always will be.

Buyers of certain types of books go into a bookstore pre-conditioned to look for or to avoid certain things. You need to know the culture of your audience. It's possible certain words or phrases have fallen into disrepute. "Water Conservation" is currently such a phrase. In the experience of people in drought stricken regions, it's been overused, misused, abused and confused. It seems that the more water people save, the higher their water bill and the greater their resentment.

Rule Ten—A "working title" is often just an expedient choice, because you have to use *something*. It can become so familiar by the time the project is over, it may seem acceptable. However, it could be far from your best choice. The working title for this book when we started was *Book Publicity that Works*. After trying several others on our "committee of experts," we decided that *Book Blitz—Getting Your Book in The News* was a lot more exciting. It always gets a strong, positive reaction when people first hear it.

Rule Eleven—Biblical or Shakespearean phrases have a certain "gravity" about them. Titles like C*hariots of Fire* from the book of *II King*s, *Inherit the Wind* from the book of *Proverbs*, or *This Above All (Hamlet)* can add familiar dignity to a title.

Rule Twelve—Legal or medical terms provide the searching author with a long list of possibilities. Attorney Scott Turow decided the phrases *Presumed Innocent* and *Burden of Proof* from courtroom jargon made good titles. Robin Cook found a best-selling title in *Coma*.

Rule Thirteen—Incompatible words make arresting titles. *Search for Red October* and *Cardinal of the Kremlin* by Tom Clancy intrigue you into buying, if only to discover what red has to do with October or what a prince of the Catholic Church is doing in Russian headquarters.

Rule Fourteen—Many phrases have become cliché, but their familiarity can work for you in a title, especially if a slight twist by word or letter substitution can enhance or even reverse its meaning. For example, D*eadly Beloved* is a reverse twist on the opening words in a marriage ceremony, "Dearly beloved..."

Rule Fifteen—Be outrageous! Marcus Meleton, an author who's quoted in chapter nine (page 130: An ABA Debriefing), used a suggestive word in his title. He called his book *Nice Guys Don't Get Laid*. Other than in the title, there's not another naughty word to be found in anything he's written. But, he realized that people like to giggle over mildly suggestive remarks. People will stop dead in their tracks and take a second look at a sexy, well-turned phrase. They just *have* to know what's inside.

Other examples, like *The Ugly Truth About Men* or *The World's Worst Bosses* promise something with which we can all relate. There's an old retail sales adage that states once a book is picked off the shelf, a high percentage of them get carried to the check-out counter. Now ask yourself, who can resist peeking between the pages of a book with an outrageous title?

Title ideas are all around us: A passing car may have a vanity license plate appropriate for a title. A line from the lyrics of a song may work because it's a phrase that's already on everyone's lips. A few words from a casual conversation or the punchline of a joke may be perfect. Even a famous title like *The Accidental Tourist* could be switched to *The Occidental Tourist* for a book about Americans visiting Japan, giving your new book a familiar sound. A slight twist to the already familiar is frequently done and is perfectly acceptable.

It pays to be constantly alert and on the lookout for word combinations, as long as you're careful not to be boring about it. Whenever an intriguing phrase pops up, grab a pen and write it down.

It's possible to find a great title first and start the book later. Books have been known to grow out of titles, and a good title can help you visualize the project as if it's done.

Dick Beals (4 feet-6 inches tall and 68 pounds) has been the voice of "Speedy" for 40 years of Alka-Seltzer television and radio commercials. He wrote his autobiography after having lived the phrase *Think BIG* all his life, so, of course, it became the title of his book. It's hard to imagine another phrase to better sum up his remarkable life.

"Promise the impossible" kind of titles carry a burden of proof. The writer dares not cheat the reader. A title like *Quick Weight Loss Without Diet or Exercise* might be rejected as nonsense. You have to back up the claim of your title. Books have been returned in disgust and frustration, with money refunded, when the promise of the title wasn't fulfilled. The title may have sold some books, but the anger of a few can seriously damage your credibility.

Gather a respected committee of associates to test your list of title ideas. Ask them to suggest their own if they have a hard time selecting one of yours.

Start a folder and label it "Titles." It can be a convenient hopper for the clever words you see or hear, the things you read and research, or just what pops into your head over a period of time. Get into the habit of writing them down and tossing them in.

Just think of it as a treasure hunt.

TYPOS:

Don't let typographical errors ruin your book. A good practice to follow is to find several well-educated friends who are willing and able to carefully proofread your manuscript or galleys and mark, in red, all the mistakes they can find. In turn, promise each of them a free autographed copy and the mention of their name, with gratitude, on the acknowledgment page.

Remember, the "spelling program" within your computer won't solve the problem. If you've typed an *if* and it was supposed to be an *of*, or an *in* instead of the word *an*, the built-in dictionary will recognize either word as correct.

The following sums up the problem rather well:

THE TYPO
The typographical error
Is a slippery thing and sly;
You can hunt 'til you are dizzy,
But it somehow will get by.

'Til the forms are off the presses
It is strange how still it sleeps;

It shrinks down in a corner,
And it never stirs nor peeps.

That typographical error
Is too small for human eyes;
'Til the ink is on the paper,
When it grows to mountain size.

The author stares with horror,
Then he grabs his hair and groans;
The copy reader drops his head
Upon his hands and moans.

The remainder of the book
May be as clean as clean can be,
But that typographical error
Is the only thing they'll sea.

Anonymous

READY, SET, GO!

To make it easy for you to coordinate your book promotion efforts, the following chapters are broken down into steps to take before your book is published and steps to take after publication. Keep in mind that it's never too early to start thinking about the promotion...even if you're still writing the book...even if you're still working on the proposal! Try writing a promotion plan for your book and add it to your book proposal. Publishers want to know that authors will be actively involved in selling the book.

The purpose of this book is to help authors improve their public relations skills, establish a timetable and delineate specific goals for successful book publication.

So put on your book promotion hat right now and continue reading!

CHAPTER TWO

A Million-Seller Book or A Million Books in Your Cellar

—Chapter Two—
Whether you're self-published or have a
trade publisher, your books will gather dust
in a warehouse cellar unsold unless a lot
of effort is put forth to reach your
reading public. What you need is a plan . . .

STEPS ONE THROUGH THREE

Prior to printing . . .

1. Refocus on your book's target audience

2. Develop a strategic plan

3. Develop a list of publications that will be interested in it

Every year, thousands of books are published and then perish. The task of getting people to walk into a bookstore, fill out a mail order form or call an 800 number, comes from a carefully engineered plan that matches the hopes and expectations of your reader.

Here are the 60 steps necessary to keep your book in the public eye. These steps have evolved at Gaughen Public Relations from years of experience promoting books and from the input of successful authors, media contacts, and publicists. The Book Publicity Seminars, which teach professionals as well as novices how to make their books irresistible to the press and public, have benefited from the development of this material.

Ask anyone who's *never* published a book and they'll all say the same thing. "Selling a book is the publisher's job. *Everybody* knows that." Everybody knows that except those who've actually had writing and publishing experience. There will never be a shortage of "those who know."

The bad news is they're wrong. The good news is that you, the author, are your book's best salesperson anyway. You're way ahead of the pack when it comes to promotion. Authors are passionate about their creations. That makes them much better salespeople than anyone at the publishing house because they believe in the inherent value of what they've produced. For every employee working for your publisher, there are 100 books in their inventory. They can't afford to worry about any but the top-listed, the few proven money makers. Only *you* really know your book's value and how to put it across. The next step is to convince your public. Here's how:

Step 1. Refocus on your book's target audience— Get to know your customer. Ask yourself, "Who will buy my book?" Start to picture the person who will benefit from your book: their psychological and social profile, their values and lifestyle. Ask yourself the following questions: What do they want or need? What do they do every day? What magazines, newspapers, newsletters, etc. do they read. What are their viewing and listening habits (TV and radio).

CASE STUDY: *A Jar of Pickles*

"What kind of a gift *do* you get for an expectant mother, besides a carton of ice cream and a jar of pickles?" pondered Don Parker, CEO of Conceivable Concepts, Inc.

Parker, 35, himself an eligible bachelor with

no practical experience in these matters, remembers how he perceived the need for *The Maternal Journal*. "I was sitting in the reception area of The Ultrasound Center (a facility Parker manages in Burbank, California) speaking with women about their pregnancy and childbirth. I asked them if they were happy with their experience so far? What would they change?

"The answers I got indicated there was no shortage of information or resources for prenatal education. However, much of what was available to read was too complex and not organized to provide the information in any kind of logical and timely order. They all joked about needing a post-graduate level of understanding," Parker said. "They also felt their doctors were too busy to talk to them in detail about it.

"So the idea came to me," he recalled. "I decided to create something fun to read, something that would be filled with helpful hints and facts in a simple format with cartoons. It could also include the essential technical and clinical tidbits, but in friendly, timely and easy-reading plain language. I knew something like that would be easy to sell to a rather large segment of the population."

Parker, and his partner Matthew Bennett, really had two target audiences—not only the pregnant woman in need of information, but also her friends who wished to give her something enjoyable, attractive and very appropriate in honor of the blessed event. What he had in mind was clearly lacking in the marketplace. What was needed was a prenatal gift item that was inexpensive yet informative, that would cover all the data without being too technical. That, he thought, should be very easy to sell.

What he created was more than a book. It was also a planner and a perpetual calendar. Its very uniqueness created a problem at first when he tried to define it for his buyers. It was, in reality, a new form of publication. He needed to insist it was a book, to avoid confusing retailers. Although it was undated, they might have been tempted to display it among their calendars, which would give it a limited "life expectancy." Since it had a unique audience, it also might have been overlooked.

Parker also found out there was a limited window of opportunity for buyers—sometime after the mother-to-be, or her friends, learn of the pregnancy usually around two months after conception and before the fifth month. After that, a book like his would be considered to be too late to be helpful. It would be like giving someone a regular calendar in August. Conceivable Concept's second book called *The Baby Journal*, which deals instead with the newborn baby, seems not to suffer from such a tight time restriction.

Along the way, Parker solved a packaging dilemma. Originally the "book" was shrink-wrapped to extend its shelf-life. However, sales plummeted, since its best selling point (the colorful cartoons and humor between its covers) was concealed. For this very same reason, when it wasn't wrapped, it suffered a lot of handling damage from those who leafed through it just for the laughs. He decided not to wrap the books when a test-market in the Midwest Baby Superstore chain sold the unwrapped stock at more than twice the volume of the wrapped stock. This test helped clarify the buying habits of his target audience.

Step 2. Develop a strategic plan—
No book can be successful without a marketing plan developed from the answer to "Why will people buy my book." You should plan carefully to position your book to serve your reader's need for information, encouragement, romance, etc. ...and keep enhancing this point in the program you develop. Some people have been successful operating from a hunch, an intuition, or their own personal preferences. Be aware that these strokes of luck are rare. With over 50,000 books published every year, don't take any chances!

Sometimes great things have been accomplished by major celebrities such as Paul Newman. In his successful ventures into food products, he donated the profits to charity. The instant name recognition due to his being a celebrity, plus his great generosity, would have made most anything he chose to produce a success.

But most of us aren't so lucky, or so well-known. We need a solid plan that will keep us from venturing off into unproductive activities, from spending money on guess-work, or from losing out on windows of opportunity because we're just not prepared for them.

Your plan should be an evolving one that continues to create a desire for your book. There will always be circumstances no one can anticipate, so it's good to review it from time to time. Keep looking for ways to let people know about your book. It usually takes at least seven "knocks on the head" to get people to progress from awareness to persuasion to buy your book. You need to plan and budget for unique and creative ways to "step in their path."

CASE STUDY: *Embracing Changes*
An excellent example of plans that change, in this case due to highly-successful sales, is the story

of the Voice Dialogue books. These books established a new method of therapy among psychologists and psychiatrists throughout the world.

Authors Hal and Sidra Stone of Albion, in northern California, both PhDs in clinical psychology, have had experience in three levels of publishing. They self-published their first book on their "Voice Dialogue" method entitled *Embracing Heaven and Earth* and had it printed and distributed by DeVorss Publishing in Marina Del Rey, California. Their next several books were published by a larger publisher, Nataraj (formerly partners in New World Library), a small specialty press located in Mill Valley, California. They are now being handled by a major publisher, Harper-SanFrancisco, the west coast office of Harper Publishing of New York City.

"We learned from all three that, in any case, you have to take ultimate responsibility for your own publicity and that it's your own energy behind the book that really makes it go," says Penny Ayeroff, Executive Director of Delos, Inc., the company that handles the doctors' seminar activities and publishing efforts.

"The amount of money spent and the publicity generated is in direct proportion to the size of the company with whom you're dealing," Ayeroff notes. "Our first 'publisher' was very good to us. DeVorss printed the book, stored it, distributed it and billed for it at our expense. They withheld a portion of every check to cover these expenses. They also charged us a modest amount for being included in their catalog. This is not a bad arrangement if you're an unknown author. But the rest of the job of publicity was up to us. What made it difficult was their name—DeVorss. It was comparatively unknown to the retail market. Now, when we speak to bookstore owners and managers, we realize the value of having the name of a major, well-known publisher like Harper behind us.

"The smaller publishers are looking for printing quantities within a certain range—there's a limit to the quantity they're set up to handle. On the plus side, they know who you are when you call, give you very personalized attention, and you don't have to sell too many books in order to be considered an important author in their eyes. Many large publishers only seem to notice you or support a publicity effort on your behalf if you make the *New York Times' Best Seller List*. Smaller companies will give you more control over editorial decisions and appearance (book layout and cover design), and can offer you a reasonable amount of support in the area of publicity. When a bookstore sets up a book signing party for you, for example, they'll often ask if your publisher will contribute toward the advertising expenses (the designing and placing of ads, the printing of posters, the preparation, printing and mailing of flyers, etc.). A small to medium-size publisher is usually flexible enough to quickly come up with the needed funds," she says.

"But, if your sales turn hot, they may lack *that* kind of flexibility. If your book really goes ballistic, as they say, the smaller publisher often lacks the capital to keep up as easily as a larger company.

"However, everything is a trade off. With a major publisher, you need to be prepared to lose a lot of creative control," Ayeroff warns. "If you regard your book as if it was your newborn child, you might experience severe withdrawal pains as they take over. It's *their* book after the contract is signed. They can change the title, design the cover, request extensive re-writes with or without your involvement and with little or no approval from you. This depends on how important they feel you are or how well you've negotiated your contract. If the changes are what their marketing department says will sell your book, you haven't much choice. They have the final word, unless, of course, your last book was the number one best seller that year. So it's essential to let go of your ego at this point."

There are advantages and disadvantages to whichever kind of publisher you choose. But when it comes to appearances, interviews, signings, or speeches to promote your book, you're the one who is in the spotlight, regardless of who's handling the bookings. You're the one who knows the most about your book. No one else can convince the person on the other end of the line as well as you can. The more you're in control and not relying on someone else, the more effective you'll be.

"Our books have special insights into self discovery and human behavior. They are recommended reading in many major universities and used by MDs and reputable psychologists and psychiatrists the world over. Unfortunately, our experiences with publicists, either from the publisher or privately hired, have been disappointing," Ayeroff says. "Unless someone is thoroughly acquainted with the psychological modalities within the Voice Dialogue technique of therapy, he or she hasn't a chance of intelligently answering a producer's or reporter's questions. There is a level of understanding, in the selling of some books, that only the author can reach.

"A larger publishing house, like Harper, can also provide media training," emphasizes Ayeroff. "Although Drs. Hal and Sidra Stone have been teachers all their professional lives and have conducted international seminars for over fifteen years, this training, nonetheless, taught them many of the subtle intricacies of performing before a camera. It's something that will continue to benefit them for the rest of their careers. This kind of training is available from a private consultant, but it can be quite expensive."

Penny Ayeroff maintains an author's greatest asset is a personal attachment to the people on the "other side" of your telephone. A friend in the publisher's publicity department can open doors and make things happen for you. On the other hand, an antagonistic approach can label you as a "difficult author," a pariah in the publishing field. It's very easy for egotistic and controlling personalities to find dozens of reasons for losing their temper when some of the contractual conditions are enforced by a major publishing house. But publishers are simply protecting your mutual interests. They'll have no time for you if you become a pain-in-the-neck. They'll just stop listening to you.

"Having started as self-publishers, Drs. Hal and Sidra Stone gradually had to let go of almost all creative control of their books as they became more and more successful. This paradox would have been very difficult for almost anyone to handle. Ironically, the very techniques of relationship psychology they write about in their books came to their rescue. Their teachings are based on understanding our 'selves' and how to control our emotions, our inner critic and our self-esteem.

"They both realized it wasn't personal," Ayeroff states. "They knew these were business decisions, and if they wanted certain results, certain things had to be controlled by the publisher."

Being able to control one's emotions also helps on personal appearance tours. "In therapy workshops, whenever possible, every attempt is made to screen participants to be sure they're stable," she explains. "For deep psychological work, we refer people out to other professionals.

But once, when Dr. Hal Stone was on a book tour in London, a member of the audience stood up and began rocking back and forth in a dance-like, fluid motion. He then moved into and down the aisle toward the stage. As Dr. Stone kept talking, the man began to remove his clothes, dropping them a piece at a time as he danced his way onto the stage. As a trained clinician, Dr. Stone knew what he was seeing, and in a calm voice asked the audience to ignore the man and let him respond and express himself in the only way he knew how. He knew he wasn't dangerous. So he minimized the distraction by calmly ignoring the incident and telling his audience to do the same.

"The man removed all but his slacks, danced his way across the rear of the stage and back into the audience, eventually returning to his seat," Ayeroff says. "Through it all, Dr. Stone managed to maintain his objectivity and the attention of his audience. Always careful not to be negative, he remained calm and sympathetic, and was later praised by many for the way he handled a disturbing situation."

Once again, anything can happen out there—but think of the fascinating stories you'll be able to tell!

REJECTION

Your plan should also anticipate rejection. It will happen whether you or someone else is the publisher. Even major publishers can't protect you from it.

There are at least three levels of rejection in publishing. If you've avoided the first rejection and your idea has been accepted by a publisher, don't think for a minute all your problems or rejections are behind you.

Rejection is not uncommon at the decision-making level, after your book's production is under way. It may not be possible for you to maintain control over the content or the cover design. The cover design and even title changes are often done "internally." The editor assigned to your book may have some strong and irreversible ideas about how you should have written it. The best advice is to listen or face the possibility of being stamped with the stigma of "the difficult author" referred to in the last Case Study.

All of this should be understandable from a business point of view. Your publisher is putting up all the money and it's their business, after all, to make a reasonable return on their investment. Middle-level management has to make proper decisions to be able to face top management after the end of the fiscal year. When it comes to business and marketing subtleties, publishers usually regard authors as non-professionals.

Another potential area of rejection is at the retail level. If the individual book buyer has never heard of you or your book, or can't understand what it's about when examining it, he probably won't purchase it for his store. With only so much money to work with, why should he buy your book instead of that of another, more familiar author?

Yet another rejection can come from your publisher's sales force. Why should they take their time to push your little book when, for three times the commission, the publisher's representatives have books in their catalog by major, well-respected authors whose books sell like hard-cover hotcakes?

CASE STUDY: *The Confusing Cover*

Ernie Weckbaugh knows rejection from first-hand experience. "Many years ago, I received my first letter of acceptance from a major eastern publisher, a company boasting over 100 million dollars in annual sales. In my mind I could already see the cover, with the title and credit *by Ernest L. Weckbaugh*. They wanted to develop my idea into a series of four illustrated books. I hadn't given much thought about how I was going to work with the publisher or how the books would be accepted. That these could become problems never passed through my mind. My hurriedly conceived suggestions for titles were quickly accepted. Too quickly in retrospect. My research in later years on effective market research testing techniques and the importance of carefully selecting the right title out of a list of many ideas, convince me now how weak those first ideas were. But, in my innocence, I had explicit faith in the publisher's creative ability.

"Since I've earned my living as a graphic designer since 1948, I thought I would have the privilege of designing the covers for my books.

However, they respectfully declined my offer, insisting that it needed to fit the overall style of their other books and would be done best by their own artists. I reluctantly backed off, placing my trust in the unknown and in the fact that these were really some of the nicest people with whom I'd ever done business. I was pleased with their cover concept. I really thought they'd created a very clever solution.

"It was only later that I realized how confusing and hard-to-sell these four books became with their misleading titles, obscure contents and ambiguous cover graphics. I watched in disappointment as people would take them off the shelf, open to a page somewhere in the middle, then invariably replace them. These were a new kind of puzzle book and I realized, too late, just how important the cover is in explaining the concept of a book, especially one with new ideas.

"I thought that my publisher would arrange for me to talk to prospective buyers. When this didn't happen, I arranged, on my own, for a chance to speak to those I thought were my target audience. I met with further rejection when I discovered them to be parents or volunteer teachers who were confused by the new learning technique I had created. As it turned out, I was dangling a difficult task in front of them and they simply weren't interested. No amount of promises, nor stories of the rewards in store for them were sufficient to sway them. It was too much work not understanding the value of the payoff. I couldn't blame them for the way they reacted. I just hadn't done my homework.

"Would I have listened to anyone who might have warned me against any of these pitfalls? I don't honestly know. Had I consulted with an expert book publicist, I certainly would have tried to identify and interview members of my target audience *before* I spent all that time and involved a publisher in spending their money printing 40,000 copies of my books. When I finally called the publisher after microscopic royalty checks began arriving every six months, they confessed they had no idea how to market my books.

"What have I learned that I can apply to my current writing projects? Now, before I spend a lot of time writing, I research my target market. Exactly who are my readers going to be? How do I find them? I interview those who could use the information in my book and ask a lot of questions. Having a thorough knowledge of my market avoids a lot of disappointment later."

Step 3. Develop a list of publications and major book reviewers that will be interested in your book— Block out the better part of a day to spend at the library with *The Literary Market Place.* Copy down the magazines and newspapers that review books of your genre. (See Book BLITZ Gray Pages for the list of the most important book review media.) You'll also find radio and television interviewers and other information you'll need later (like book distributors, book clubs and support services). Whether you use index cards or a computer, put the information in a form that's easy for you to find and to update as you go along.

CHAPTER THREE

Cast
That Net...
Beat
That Drum!

—Chapter Three—
Begin developing your network of
media people and persistently
beat the drums for your book.

STEPS FOUR THROUGH SIX

Prior to printing . . .

4. Send bound galleys and query letters to selected editors

5. Prepare media release reporters will read and publish

6. Send out your media release as needed for newsworthy items

Step 4. Send bound galleys and query letters to selected editors—

This is one of the most important mailings you can do if you want reviews from the major media reviewers. Use a message that shows you know each publication's target audience. Read these publications often and if you're not sure about review policies, call and ask. The editors are almost always very helpful and willing to answer questions. Be sure to double check the name and spelling of the editor and organization with a phone call to their receptionist. Getting a letter addressed to his or her predecessor is considered unprofessional.

"The biggest mistake anyone can make, even among professionals, is to write the news release first before they talk to anyone in the media—reporters, editors, talk-show producers," according to Elisabeth Handler, president of The Handler Group, Communications and Marketing, of Burbank, California, and lecturer on public relations at the University of Southern California. She suggests you call directly to anyone you hope will be using your story. Ask the secretary or operator to put you through to the person who'll be receiving your news release. Double check the spelling of their name and ask if you have the proper address, zip code, etc. Ask them if they'd rather have you fax or mail your news release to them.

While you have them on the line, pick their brain as much as you can without overdoing it. This is your *golden opportunity* to explain what you have. Ask what they want and what they don't want you to include, is there a preferred format, and what else they might be interested in having before you send it to them.

During your brief and friendly conversation, while you still have their attention, tell them about a newsworthy issue that relates to the book, how that applies to your personal background, and especially how it relates to the audience you're trying to reach. Listen to their response and do what they say. Let them know you're trying to help them do their job. Then, when you follow up the next week by phone to ask if they've received your material, they'll already know you. A preliminary contact and your willingness to follow their procedure greatly multiplies your chances of motivating them to use it when it comes.

Be prepared. If your book is on divorce, know your statistics. Is divorce up, is it on the decline, and what percentage of the population is affected by it? Is your message relevant to what's happening today? If you've done your homework, your contact will know it and appreciate it.

But you have to choose the media correctly. If you're an expert on gardening, you shouldn't be talking to the editor of the *L.A. Times* or the *New York Times* Business Section. With a little research, you'll find out that there is a radio station KCRW in Santa Monica, California, for example, which has a regular Friday afternoon garden show for a call-in audience. That's the place and the person you should be calling. Here is a 100 percent pre-qualified listening audience. Your story written up in the *Times* View Section may reach a million and one people, but you can't be sure one million and one of them really care.

How do you find this little station in this small-to-medium-sized town? Find a good media directory from your public library or call the local chapter of the Public Relations Society of America. Public relations industry targeted directories, such as *Bacon's* or *Gebbie's All-in-One,* give a detailed listing of this kind of information. They list publications, radio and TV shows that deal with every kind of human interest and activity known to man—from animal husbandry, to jewelry, to pipe fitting, to zinnia gardening.

Reduced advertising budgets put the news media under more pressure than ever before. The space for news in the newspapers has shrunk along with these budgets. Even TV talk shows no longer support large research staffs. So be prepared to give responding reporters a complete story, not one that requires more research on their part. Don't give them a tiny piece of a story...do your homework. Provide a thorough and well-rounded story so that any producer or writer can simply pick it up and run with it.

Make it fit. Watch the TV show and read the newspaper or magazine with an analytical eye. Ask yourself,

"What is it they're looking for?" Talk to someone in the business who can advise you on the editorial content of certain shows or the requirements of certain sections of a newspaper. Remember, from their unsung position in the eye of the storm, secretaries and receptionists are often well informed and eager to please.

Details matter to people who deal with words. The written word sent writer to writer must be letter perfect. It is essential that grammar, spelling and punctuation be correct. It's worth *everything* to you to have your correspondence carefully proofread, otherwise you are discredited and your message will never get through. There is just too much competition and too much money involved to expect anyone to indulge you.

Step 5. Prepare a news release that newspaper reporters and TV or radio producers will read—
A news release should always be sent with review copies and with requests for review tear sheets (from newspapers). A well-written release should tell a story and talk about the benefits of reading your book. If possible, tie its content into current events that are happening in the news. Keep it to one page, double spaced.

Chances are a well-written press release, for a small, local newspaper, will probably be run "as is." A similar one, sent to the *New York Times,* may be only a gesture to catch a reporter's attention or a quick glance. What are your chances it will be printed verbatim? Not very good. Send a "pitch letter" instead, much like the query letter you might send to a publishing house. The pitch letter is a teaser. It says, "Here's who I am, and here's what I've got...are you interested in knowing more?" Where the news release tells the whole story, the pitch letter entices. You want reporters or editors to finish it thinking, "I'd really like to know more about that." What you say must be clear, not confusing, cute or enigmatic. You don't want to irritate, you just want to be intriguing enough for someone to pick up the phone and call you for the rest of the story.

A news release that gets noticed is straight forward in its content. Any attempt to mimic the elaborate style of the publication to which you're submitting may be resented. You risk sounding coy, cute or even sarcastic by doing what might be considered a parody of a certain writer's style. Just tell the facts and let the reporter adjust the style and add the decorative words.

In order to interest the press you must offer something they consider to be news, according to publicist Tena Spears of First Impressions (Portland, Oregon). You need to assess the appeal of your book. Is it important? Does it have strong human interest appeal? Does it have national appeal? Does it have a strong "hard news" hook? Is there a celebrity connection?

CASE STUDY: *Doctor, Heal Thy Penmenship*

While working on a promotional campaign for a book on handwriting improvement, Spears approached the *American Medical Association News* and suggested they do an article on doctors and their handwriting. In addition to suggesting the story, she provided names and phone numbers of doctors who had used the program successfully. After the article appeared, over 2,000 doctors called to order the book!

In this case, since doctors are notorious for their poor handwriting, the fact that they were using the program with great success *was* news! The fact they were even *interested* in doing something about their penmanship was news! The result: One article in the *AMA News* enabled her to attract the attention of *People Magazine, The Los Angeles Times, The Sunday Express*

*(London), The National Herald Tribune, and
Library Journal,* as well as local and regional
television news stations.

Does your book have an interesting history? Is it being
used as a text? Has your book caused a controversy or has
it been the focus of public attention? If it hasn't, then
make something happen.

Step 6. Send out the news release—
Use the list you've developed from *The Literary Market
Place,* but don't neglect your local media. Be sure that you
let them know you are a hometown person who's done
something newsworthy.

Several other publications are available to help you
find the right people to contact for regional and national
publications. Among them are Power Media "Selects."
They are available from:
Broadcast Interview Source
2233 Wisconsin Ave., N.W.
Washington, D.C. 2007-4104
Phone: (202) 333-4904 or Fax: (202) 342-5422

CASE STUDY: *Scaring Up Public Appearances*
"Consistently sending out news releases to
radio stations, newspapers and appropriate magazines requesting that they interview you or write
an article about your book can reap huge rewards,"
says Aaron Silverman, president of SCB Distributors of Gardena, California. "There is one author I
work with who writes books on 'fear.' He makes
sure he's booked on radio or television talk shows
and covered by the press every Friday the 13th and
Halloween. He then sends a list of where he's been
written up and interviewed to his book distributor
and their salesmen. Such a small effort can make

an amazing difference in book sales."

CASE STUDY: Fire Chiefs to the Rescue

Emily Dee, author of *Souls on Board*, admits she sabotaged herself earlier in her career by not marketing and promoting her book aggressively. She simply didn't realize the value of the press.

Her book is about the airline disaster of Flight 232, which crashed short of the runway in her home town of Sioux City, Iowa, on July 19, 1989. In it, she deals with both the primary trauma of the passengers and the secondary trauma of their families' grief. Her emphasis is on preparedness, panic control and Post-Traumatic Stress Syndrome.

Since her book had such an urgent news orientation, she decided to self-publish and not wait for the minimum of 18 to 24 months that most trade publishers normally take.

"But, when it came to promoting my book, I simply didn't know what to do," she confessed. "However, books like the *Complete Guide to Self-Publishing: Everything You Need to Know to Write, Publish, Promote and Sell Your Own Book* by Tom and Marilyn Ross ultimately came to my rescue.

"Doing it by myself, I became keenly aware of the ever-present need for marketing," she said. "At a Santa Barbara, California workshop for Emergency Response and Disaster Preparedness, I met a book reviewer from *Rescue Magazine*. The article she wrote about my book brought in countless orders from fire chiefs across the country.

"While I was in Santa Barbara, I attended Dan Poynter's workshop on self-publishing. He's the author of *The Self-Publisher's Manual: How to Write, Print and Sell Your Book*. Like the Ross' book, it was a marvelous guide and helped to set me on the right path. Dan has since become a good friend and a valued marketing consultant.

"While I was in Santa Barbara, I met Barbara Gaughen and attended her book publicity workshop the next day on Monday.

"I also discovered the Publishers Marketing Association. They've been wonderful in sending out mailings to bookstores and reviewers, staging group exhibits and organizing co-op mailings. I've learned so much from them about what I'm supposed to be doing.

"I've also had opportunities to speak at several seminars," she said. "A public appearance at an appropriate event with a supply of your books conveniently available is absolutely critical to sales momemtum. It's essential to link your promotional appearances with your distribution efforts. Be sure the fulfillment people know when and where you need books. This is true if you're self-published or if you have a major publisher.

"Promotion can be a real problem if you're shy about meeting people or appearing in front of the public. Self-publishers have only themselves to rely on when it comes to selling their book.

"However, this situation is equally true for writers who are fortunate enough to have a trade publisher behind them," she noted. "It doesn't really make a lot of difference whether you or someone else publishes the book, you're going to be on the front line battling for sales either way. So you'd better be preparing yourself now to enjoy it. It's something that can be learned, is very exciting, satisfying and highly creative, and is a very large part of what you, as an author, have chosen to do."

In 1992, an ABC Television movie was made based on the events depicted in Emily Dee's book. It was entitled *"Crash Landing—The Rescue of Flight 232"* and it starred Charlton Heston, Richard Thomas and James Coburn.

CHAPTER FOUR

The Paper Boomerang

—Chapter Four—
Send out the summary of your
book to reviewers and make
it easy for them to respond.

STEPS SEVEN THROUGH TWELVE

Prior to printing . . .

7. Develop a brochure or flyer

8. Send a brochure/flyer with a "bounce-back" to reviewers

9. Participate in "Books for Review"

10. Compile a list of targeted organizations

11. Phone organizations to discuss offer to members

12. Send out brochure/flyer to direct mail audience

The activities in this segment are best scheduled two months prior to publication. They require intense telephone contact and public speaking. If you ever enjoyed acting or speaking up in class, now is the time to recapture that feeling.

On the other hand, if talking to a stranger on the telephone scares you silly, don't wait until the last two months to take action. Sign up now for an appropriate course through Adult Education, join Toastmasters or

start speaking up at PTA. Volunteer for a charity telephone drive where they'll teach you solicitation techniques. Compared to calling for donations in this tough
economy, talking to the press will be a breeze.

Step 7. Develop a book brochure or flyer—
This can be as simple as an 8-1/2" by 11" sheet of paper
or as elaborate as your budget will allow. It should
include a synopsis of the book, a brief biography, your
photo, the fact that you are available for interviews,
your address and phone number. Add quotes about the
book from experts in the field or other authors and
quotes about your speaking ability.

This is no time to be modest about your accomplish-
ments or the benefits of reading your book. Use attention-grabbing sentences right from the start.

The meek shall not inherit Donahue

Instead of saying a mouthful like, "This is a satirical
book about the serious subject of why women go for men
who treat them badly," author Marcus Meleton took a
shorter, more attention-grabbing approach. Following
the encourgement of Gwen Carden, whose work has
appeared in publications as diverse as American Woman
and the National Enquirer, he started with the headline, "Why Do Jerks Attract Women?"

His first paragraph told the story of why he wrote
the book: "Marcus Pierce Meleton, Jr. went to a party
and watched as the biggest jerk at the party left with
four women. This was the spark that ignited his book,
Nice Guys Don't Get Laid."

Also gracing the page was an illustration from the
book that brought home his topic. It's a "nice guy"
bringing flowers to a young woman whose body language and facial expression show she's less than interested in his offering. The young man stands with his

back to us. On his back is a sign that reads, "Scrape Shoes HERE."

That's what it takes to get through all the confusion and clutter of unsolicited material on a reviewer's desk. Anything less is an invitation for a quick trip to the "round file."

Step 8. Send out your brochure or flyer with a "bounce back" post card to reviewers— A "bounce back" post card (business reply card) is the easiest way for those who are interested in reviewing your book to be in touch with you. The post card has a return address with pre-paid postage on one side and a book review request on the other side. The book review request should ask informational questions about the name of their publication/broadcast station, circulation, audience profile, contact and their mailing address.

Reviewers will mark what they want and reply by your "bounce back" card.

Step 9. Participate in books for review— Twice yearly Publishers Marketing Association mails a catalog of 38 book titles to major newspapers with each book categorized, a photo of the book cover and a 100-word description. Call them for the current cost of this service.

Send book category, cover photo and description to:
Publishers Marketing Association
2401 Pacific Coast Highway, #102
Hermosa Beach, CA 90254
Phone: (310) 372-2732
Fax: (310) 374-3342

Step 10. Compile a list of targeted organizations or businesses that may want you as a guest speaker or will help sell your book—
One way of attracting the press and generating interest in your book is to offer a free workshop or seminar. Newspapers will readily announce free seminars and workshops. All you have to do is make sure your news release gets to the right person on time.

The authors of the handwriting improvement book mentioned in chapter 3 hold a seminar every January. This year the workshop was attended by over 350 people. One caution: Do not make buying your book a requirement for entry into the workshop, but they can certainly be available in the back of the room for purchase. Incidentally, having a large crowd attend your workshop is news, use it. Let the press know the number of participants you expect prior to the event!

Check your local Chamber of Commerce list of local organizations. Go to the library's reference desk for the Directory of Associations for regional, state or national contacts.

Another source is *The Encyclopedia of Associations,* which has an *index* volume close to four inches thick. The other two main volumes of listings are each twice that big. Nearly all of these associations send out newsletters to their avid readers. Whatever your book is about, it has an existing audience somewhere in one of these association or media volumes. If you're looking for your market; an advertising medium for your book; a sponsor of your book; an audience for a speech about your book—everyone and anyone of importance to you can quickly be found somewhere within those pages and easily contacted. This could be the beginning of a never-ending network of contacts. Success with even a few of them gains the attention of the many you ultimately want to reach.

Non-profit and civic groups, even businesses and book stores, are often hungry for new speakers. Prepare a list of two or three book-related topics with which you feel comfortable. Some organizations might also be willing to sell your book through their newsletter if they receive some of the profits.

CASE STUDY: *The Miracle Writer*

Caring for young children is a full-time job for almost anyone, including author Joni Hilton. However, with four children ages one to eleven, Hilton is also a professional writer, a former Miss California, and she holds a masters degree from the University of Southern California.

Other than her seven books, she writes humorous articles for women's magazines (*Family Circle, McCall's, Woman's Day, Parents*) and is in demand as a speaker as much as her busy schedule will allow. She also produces audio tapes of her books.

Hilton has had a considerable amount of experience before the television camera, anchoring a TV news program for a CBS affiliate in Sacramento. She also hosted a half-hour talk show for four years on cable television, Channel 52, after she moved to the Southern California area. She has interviewed everyone from the local fire chief to major celebrities.

One morning following a trip to the orthodontist with her oldest child, Hilton spent the afternoon at the Northridge Mall in the west end of Southern California's San Fernando Valley.

But she was not there to shop...she was there to demonstrate her newest book. Surrounded by an eager audience of parents, children and colorful toys in the Imaginarium store, she opened a copy of her *Five Minute Miracles: 373 Quick Daily Projects for You and Your Kids to Share* and asked a mother and daughter to participate in one of her *Miracle* projects.

How was this latest publicity event at the Imaginarium arranged? It began at the American Booksellers Association Convention in Los Angeles in May of 1992. While attending the booth of her publisher, Running Press of Philadephia, PA, Hilton was approached by the Imaginarium people who asked if she would come to their stores and show their customers how these *Miracles* work. This is an example of a business using an author as a speaker to promote their stores. She was delighted to oblige, and has since demonstrated in eight of their stores, which are located in major malls and shopping centers throughout the Greater Los Angeles and Orange County area.

The Imaginarium's management was looking for an attraction to draw people in. Joni Hilton was looking for people to buy her books. Everyone was happy, especially her publisher. This was truly a "win-win" situation.

"This is a lot of fun to do," she says. "My book is full of ideas to show how a parent and a child can really enjoy working and learning together. Since each project is so short, it allows quite a few people to get involved in the hour or so I'm there. I'm also pleased to be surrounded by other educational products. There are toys that make art and science come alive for children and satisfy their curiosity. These are products that would satisfy any parent's desire to buy something worthwhile for their children, including my books.

"While I'm there, we usually get through six or seven projects. I need time to entertain my audience so they're in a good mood. I explain what the book is about and what some of the projects are. I give them what they need and let them do it. We have a lot of laughs from beginning to end, I sell a lot of my books, and everyone walks away happy," she says.

"I find myself *always* writing," she explains. "I take mental or written notes on everything I see or hear at the demonstrations or elsewhere as I try to keep up with my schedule. Much of it eventually finds a place in a book or an article. It can be a spoken phrase, a character I meet, an idea for a new book, an interesting situation, or something in the news.

"This is also true when it comes to promoting my books. Every other moment, when I'm not thinking about future writing projects, I'm thinking about how to let the public know about what I've already published."

To promote her books, she just gave over-the-phone interviews to several radio stations in Texas, Los Angeles and Seattle. One was an afternoon show where the host brought his own children to the interview, and another was a morning show where the hostess spoke to her mostly about parenting. One woman interviewer wanted to contact her monthly to share project ideas.

"I also enjoy just walking into a bookstore, unannounced, and getting to know the owner," she says. "A brief conversation, a one-minute demonstration of my book, a suggested booksigning or *Miracle* demonstration, a commitment from them and a handshake can, over a period of time, accumulate a lot of orders for my publisher."

She compares exercising to the need for publicizing her books. "It's something every author knows they should do" she says, "but unless it's done regularly, your sales will suffer and die in the long run.

"But promotional opportunities, like exercise, don't need to be painful. They can be fun," she points out. "You just have to find the publicity things you enjoy doing, find an easy way to do the other things and establish a time to do at least one of each consistently every day."

Step 11. Call organizations to discuss your offer to serve as a guest speaker—
Before you take out the list you've compiled and get ready to start dialing, prepare a brief description of your book and its benefits to the organization's members. You'll also need two or three book-related themes as speech topics. Don't depend on your memory. Write it all down and keep the information in front of you when you call.

If you have friends in local organizations, call them first to "test market" your calling technique. Then don't be surprised if you have to call two or three people within an organization. Be patient until you reach the person who schedules speakers.

If there's interest, follow-up with your book brochure or flyer. Put it in an envelope the minute you get off the phone. Be sure to include a note thanking the person for their time. Write on the outside of the envelope, "Enclosed is the information you requested."

Then make another call.

As soon as an organization schedules you as a speaker, contact the newspaper in their area, send them a release and your photo. See next page for an example.

Step 12. Send out your book brochure (or flyer) to the direct mail audience—
Start with family, friends, business associates and include on your mailing list anyone and everyone who might buy your book for themselves or as a gift. If your book speaks to a specific profession, hobby, interest or special interest group, targeted mailing lists can be purchased. Before spending your money, check into the longevity of the company and ask how they will compensate you for returned mail due to outdated addresses.

Direct mail produces quick response and is an inexpensive way to test your letter, bounce-back card and brochure. You can quickly change your promotion and mail again. You have complete control of your personalized advertising message.

BUSINESS

Oxnard Press-Courier   **Tuesday, July 13, 1993**

PR pro tells how to make news

By HELEN REYNOLDS
Press-Courier Staff Writer

OXNARD — For those seeking newspaper publicity, it's wise to stay current on what appeals to its subscribers, a public-relations pro says.

"Learn to recognize windows of opportunity," said public-relations specialist Barbara Gaughen.

She will be keynote speaker for the Port Hueneme Chamber of Commerce at a breakfast meeting at 7:30 a.m. Wednesday in the Lobster Trap Restaurant at Channel Islands Harbor.

If a local business is involved in measures to correct some problem making front-page news in a local newspaper, she said, it might be a good opportunity for publicity.

The owner or manager should recognize the chance to contact the news department, she said.

"Try to create relationships with people in the media and call them when you have something that might really be interesting to their audience," she said.

"If you're calling the Oxnard Press-Courier, for example, be ready to say why you think the Press-Courier and its readers can benefit."

Gaughen said fill-in-the-form press releases from a national or international headquarters, sent to local branch managers for resubmission as

their own, are unlikely to be published later if they fail to get used the first time.

"Old news releases that don't work the first time aren't likely to work the second, third, fourth — or ever," she said.

And even those that did get used the first time cannot be relied upon again, she said.

"Quit sending in the same old thing and praying," she advised. "Read the newspaper. Pay attention to the media. If you can create relationships with people in the media, they're very likely to tell you what interests them and their subscribers."

Gaughen, who heads Gaughen Public Relations in Santa Barbara, said she will describe 10 important public-relations strategies and when each might be used effectively.

People in business and industry need to learn why some aspects of their work that excite them may seem boring to others, including media representatives, while they may not recognize something they deal with daily that could be very interesting, Gaughen said.

"Be truly who you are," Gaughen said she advises her clients and seminar audiences. "You can show your customers and the media that you're interesting."

Barbara Gaughen's photo was also printed by the Oxnard Press-Courier

CHAPTER FIVE

Our Next Guest . . .

—Chapter Five—
You're on the air—whether they're talking
about you or your book, you're speaking to
them on the telephone, speaking into a
microphone or staring into a camera...

STEPS THIRTEEN THROUGH FIFTEEN

Prior to printing . . .

13. Prepare press kit

14. Phone major TV shows

15. Send press kits to interested TV shows

It's time to prepare to step out into the spotlight. Think of your unseen but eager public *awaiting* you.

Step 13. Prepare a Press Kit—

The press kit is simply a 9"x12" pocket folder which gives the media more information about you and your book and usually includes:

- Your book brochure (or flyer)
- An interesting news release
- Your photo
- Photo or reprint of the book cover (if completed)
- Your resume, bio or professional profile
- Articles that have been written about you or other books you have written

A press kit should be provocative and can be customized for a reporter/editor. If your opener is a 17-page, single-spaced document, you're lost before you start. Nobody has the time or inclination to work that hard. Only if your headline is "Cure For Cancer Found," will they consider giving it some attention. Ninety-nine percent of what comes across an editor's desk is not *that* compelling, so the contest is to work through the barriers they set up.

Your press kit format must be easily understood. Arrange your main story in outline form, using bold subheads and lists with "bullets" preceding each item on the list. Your back-up material should be a photo of you, the author, and copies of other articles or reviews written about the book. Make it "modular" so than it can serve several purposes. This flexibility means that you can pick and choose the contents depending on the audience it's going to.

The other purpose of a press kit is to provide detailed background material to support the easy-reading main outline. Fact sheets of the geographical background, the historical data, maps, diagrams, etc., which may be more than you'll ever expect to see on the final printed page, are there if the reporter should choose to use them.

Your press kit should not be written like a sales brochure. The members of the media are very suspicious of material which is too "hard-sell." Sometimes the more expensive, slick, cleverly die-cut, gold-foiled, blind-embossed, award-winning press kit folder falls flat. It can have the unfortunate effect of discounting itself as a serious source of news.

CASE STUDY: *Strike While It's Hot!*
An example of a highly successful press kit for a book on ridesharing was a blank white, off-

the-shelf, 9-1/2"x11-1/2" pocket folder. It was filled with the appropriate inserts and had a simple rubber-stamped message about seven inches long on an angle across the cover that said "Transit Strike Info" in bold red letters. It was timed to be mailed out the week before an impending local bus strike. It reviewed the book and told where copies could be purchased. The folders cost less than a dollar each in quantity and the rubber stamp was just a few dollars. The same stamp was also used on 9" x 12" white envelopes in additional mailings. The press received it as hot news and acted immediately on every submission.

PHOTO TIPS

Your photo should be a recent black and white print taken by a professional. Look at other book jackets to choose a style. Choose a photographer who will let you make your own reprints. This will allow you to make a large quantity of prints at wholesale rates in minimum time without bothering the photographer. Quantity photo printers can be found in the business section of your telephone book.

All you need is the negative to make the hundreds of prints you'll need to send with your review copies and press kits. By contrast, a professional photographer will send it out to a quantity photo lab and mark up the price to cover his cost of handling. This could take several days. If you should happen to need prints in a hurry, he may even be on assignment and unavailable. It's worth checking with your local One-Hour Photo Service. Sometimes they will take the photo for you, develop it in an hour and give you the negative, all at a very low cost compared to a professional photographer.

Your prints needn't be 8"x10" size; 4"x5" is acceptable for just about any newspaper or magazine. Identify yourself and the name of your book on the back of your photo with a business card, sticker or typed sheet taped to the back. NEVER write on the back of a photo with a pen or pencil. Your imprint will show through across the front when reproduced. If you *must* write on it for any reason, use a narrow-point felt-tip marker and write carefully along the edge.

This may seem like an obvious statement, but when writing a news release, be sure what you write qualifies as *news*.

"What *is* news?" asks Tom Miller, currently Executive Director of the Glendale Community Foundation. Following his years as the westside editor for the Los Angeles Herald Examiner, he gained extensive experience in corporate public relations as well as writing for and editing several other news publications. His wife, Susanne Whatley, is a news anchor for radio station KFI in Los Angeles, California.

"Certainly a major athlete or actor announcing that he has AIDS is news. A war that involves U.S. troops, the elections, and what your city council decides, are all news items," he points out. "But you and your book can *also* be news."

To understand what gets reported in a periodical, Miller explains there are three components to the space in any modern newspaper: 1) advertising, 2) news, and 3) advertising that looks like news. Advertising is printed after the space has been paid for by the seller of a product or service. News is placed in the paper because it is a public event or occurrence that would be of interest to a large number of readers. Advertising that looks like news (public relations) is submitted by the seller of a product or a service in the form of a news release, and it has news-like interest for many readers.

It's also important to know who decides what is

news. The news editor does that, and his or her decisions vary depending on how much space is available.

Why does the amount of space play a role in whether a story gets reported or not? It's because the quarter you put into the street rack doesn't really pay for the paper. Advertising does. Generally, 60 percent of the paper must be allocated for advertising, 40 percent for the news.

But there *are* some tricks to getting the media to pay attention to you and your book. It has a lot to do with properly preparing a news release.

A good news release is a concise, complete description of an upcoming news event like a press conference announcing the release of your book; a timely report of that event after the fact; or other news items or feature article possibilities that could tie into the news value of your book.

Initially, it's important to read the publications to which you wish to send a release. See what kind of stories they cover, what type of photography they run. Then assess if your information would be newsworthy to their readers. If it affects only a small portion of the population, you might want to rethink your efforts. If, on the other hand, a majority of their readers would be benefited by your book, then go for it.

One—Identify. Some writers label these mailings "News" or "Release" or "Media Release." This is usually printed flush left at the top of the first page. If you're seeking broadcast coverage (TV or radio), avoid the word "press" as in Press Release.

Two—Headline. Center it three or four inches below the "Release" so an editor has room to write some comments. The head should be attention-getting and truthful. Instead of heading a story "John Jones Speaks," try "Jones Takes on Council."

Three—Location and date. Enter the city and

today's date on the first line of the release.

Four—Simplify and clarify. Make your first draft as clear and concise as possible. Put the most important or attention-getting sentence first. Drop redundant phrases and forget the flowery language.

"During my days as an editor," Miller recalls, "I spent a lot of time weeding through scores of releases each week. There were few things that would get my rejection feelers twitching faster than a verbose paragraph like:

'Eloquently-prepared writers convene weekly at Writers Anonymous in a sophisticated forum to strut their stuff. The prevailing camaraderie assists participating scribblers to cherish each opportunity to verbally display their creative compositions and take note of the attendant critical comments.'

"You're much better off," Miller suggests, " just giving the meat of your message in simple, straight-forward language and avoiding the clever clichés."

Keep your release to one page whenever possible. If a second page is necessary, place a one-word headline and page number flush left at the top of the page two.

Always keep in mind that editors and reporters are looking for the facts up front. After you've given them the facts, then, and only then, will they want extra information for "fleshing out" the story.

Be thinking of the five questions all journalists are taught: Who, when, where, what, and how. Be sure to discuss these five pieces of information in the first or second paragraph, or if you are inviting media coverage of an event, they could even be made into a list.

Miller suggests adding a bit of "color" to your re-lease, such as some quotes from an authority on your book's subject or some pertinent historical data. It will sometimes pique an editor's interest. But avoid jargon not in common use unless your release is destined for trade papers only.

Five—Indicate the person to contact. Always include the name and phone number of somebody available to provide more information to a reporter. This should be typed either at the beginning or at the end of the release.

A couple of final tips: If you want to look like a pro, end each page that's going to continue with "— more—" centered at the bottom. At the end of the release, type either "—30—" or "—x x x—." Either of these are a journalist's way of ending a story.

Also, it may seem trivial, but neatness and spelling count. A release with smudges, misspellings and poor grammar or punctuation can discredit you and your information in the eyes of an editor. You *must* establish a reputation for quality information, because many small community papers or broadcast media will use good-quality releases as is, just as you submit them. If they require heavy editing, you'll seldom, if ever, see them in print or on the air.

Remember, your news release is competing with a lot of others. Everything is opened, read and evaluated for importance to the readers, listeners or viewers. A

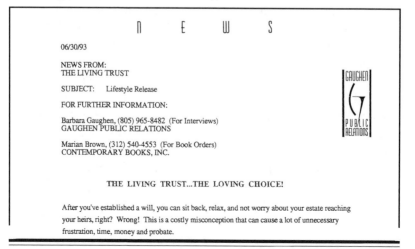

N E W S

06/30/93

NEWS FROM:
THE LIVING TRUST

SUBJECT: Lifestyle Release

FOR FURTHER INFORMATION:

Barbara Gaughen, (805) 965-8482 (For Interviews)
GAUGHEN PUBLIC RELATIONS

Marian Brown, (312) 540-4553 (For Book Orders)
CONTEMPORARY BOOKS, INC.

GAUGHEN
PUBLIC
RELATIONS

THE LIVING TRUST...THE LOVING CHOICE!

After you've established a will, you can sit back, relax, and not worry about your estate reaching your heirs, right? Wrong! This is a costly misconception that can cause a lot of unnecessary frustration, time, money and probate.

phone call to the editor or producer may help get your information accepted. But keep your call short and on the subject of your release.

Never, repeat *NEVER* bother to call after the event (a book signing, a personal appearance, etc.) wanting to find out why your release wasn't run. The answer will always be the same, "There wasn't room (or time)."

You and your book are news. Make it your task to try to prove it and make editors, producers and the reading or viewing public believe you.

Step 14. Phone television interview show producers—

First watch, read and listen to the local media before you start to contact them and before you start contacting the national media. Get a sense of the kind of stories they're likely to produce. Some look for humor, others for local angles on national stories. Your job is to tie the content of your book into their style or into a genuinely newsworthy event. For practice and a real "grassroots" start, watch your local cable access channel and note if any of the hosts bring in guest authors or experts.

If they do book guests, this is your chance to practice personalizing your press kit to match the show. Phone calls are essential. You may find it easier to phone when you have a genuine compliment for the producer of the show. Quickly give them the compliment and get on with your brief three-to-four-sentence pitch.

The more you call, the more television appearances you'll get. Be persistent! Send news items of interest about your book every two weeks. You'll be keeping in touch and have another good reason to call. Set aside time every other week to go through the routine.

Several publications are available to help you find the right people to contact for regional and national media. Talk Show "Selects" for broadcast interviewers are available from:

Broadcast Interview Source
2233 Wisconsin Ave., N.W.
Washington, D.C. 2007-4104
Phone: (202) 333-4904
Fax: (202) 342-5422

CASE STUDY: *Patience, Persistence Pay Off*

"I typically spend long days on the telephone with media people on behalf of clients. I know that a positive attitude, perseverance and a well-developed list of benefits almost always get immediate attention from the media.

"Hello. This is Barbara Gaughen in Santa Barbara, California.' Before I say that to anyone, however, I have already gone through a routine that helps prepare me for calls across the country.

"I live on the West Coast, so here is what I have to do to organize my thoughts and get ready for my calls to the eastern half of the country at the beginning of *their* business day.

"I get up in the dark and go for a walk or a jog. During this quiet time, I practice my 30-second pitch for one of my client's books. Around 6:00 a.m., I start my phone calls and as soon as I say 'This is Barbara Gaughen in Santa Barbara, California,' I have their attention and we're off. Sometimes I mention I just got back from jogging if I really want to get their attention.

"Some phone calls take 20 seconds, others last as long as 20 minutes," Gaughen notes. "I always finish my calls east of Rockies by 9:00 a.m. From 9:00 a.m. until noon, I call people located on the Pacific Coast. I systematically note the outcome of each call in writing. Then I record each note on my computer or on index cards. This includes the time I called, who answered, the results and the follow-up. I start at the top, the most important part of my list. If I want the *New York Times,* I *start* with the *New York Times.*

"Most book editors and reviewers will tell me their shelves are stacked with books waiting to be read, so I have to sell the book and its benefits. It's up to me to make it sizzle enough to get reviewed.

"When they say they don't do that kind of book review, I never hang up. I ask who might be reviewing this kind of a book and I call them immediately. I always say that 'so-and-so' said to call and begin my pitch again with them.

"After lunch," Gaughen says, "it's back on the phone and the all-important follow-up faxes, press kits and notes. I always review my notes and keep my promises from my morning calls. For every booking I get, I send a thank you fax confirming time and location."

For a free 'thank you' fax sample, call 1-805-96 FAX IT from your fax machine and order #105.

15. Send Press Kits to interested TV shows— Follow the example from Step 12. Television talk shows sell books. They take lead time and close contact with TV producers. It starts with a "pre-call" (see Step 14) to determine if they're interested in your particular subject. If the answer is yes, mail or Federal Express your press kit and videotape (if you have one) on the same day and write a message on the outside of the envelope. To attract attention, pay a visit to a gift or novelty store and see if you're able to find a sticker or rubber stamp that matches the subject of your book and use it. Next, start your phone calls within a week after they receive your press kit. You may have to call several times to secure a booking. Don't ignore local television and don't be afraid of the national shows.

SPECIAL SECTION
What happens if you land an interview?

Media experts recommend the help of an experienced media trainer. However, you might first try spending time with friends watching people being interviewed on the television news. Ask what it is about them that makes them believable? Discuss why you trust one person and not another? Do they fail to look the interviewer in the eye? What about people who shift around, or wring their hands, or sit in a slumped posture when they talk? After you've discussed the television interview, try to role play a typical interview with your friends.

Don't try humor. Accept the fact that you're going to be the straight-man in any of these encounters. Let your interviewer get the laughs if he or she can. Don't even think of competing. Comedy is a very hard act to do well.

Make a list of the most difficult, challenging or hostile questions that may come up. Assume that your host is going to try to embarrass you. He or she knows that a good story is one that's controversial. Anticipate what will be asked. What are the 25 things you *don't* want to talk about, the ones you're afraid might be asked? Figure out a way to answer them diplomatically, or dodge them without being too transparent about it. You don't *have* to answer trick questions, but you should be prepared for them so you won't appear rattled when they pop up.

Don't assume your host knows anything about your subject. He or she probably hasn't read your book, and has only heard about you a few minutes before you go on the air. Memorize a two-minute, clear explanation of the book and why it's important for everyone to buy and read. What happens if your uninformed host turns to you and says, "So, what's up?" Don't depend on anyone to draw your book out of you. You should be there, ready to give a clear and to-the-point summary.

"One of the biggest issues facing our nation today is..." starts your response, giving your host a few minutes to listen and get acquainted with your subject. Hopefully, he or she will begin forming an intelligent follow-up question as you speak. Be sure you've also memorized the three or four most important aspects of your book. Be determined to get these points across to the listening audience no matter what your host says.

What is it the audience needs to know?

• Benefit statement: Everyone will be better off if they rush out to buy your book for the following reasons...

• Call to action: It's available *now* in every bookstore across the United States.

These facts should quickly become permanently etched in your mind. Make your time there count.

We've all been trained to present our evidence and then come to a conclusion. This is absolutely wrong if you're being interviewed. Start with your conclusion. Then, if there's time, you can back it up with supportive and persuasive evidence. If you've done any news writing or feature writing, you know that your "lead" or conclusive statement comes first, then you continue your story with the rest of the facts in order of diminishing importance. It's vital for a good interview that the first words out of your mouth be the most important as well as the most interesting ones you have to say. Listeners, like readers, spend only a split-second wondering whether they really want to hear what you're saying or decide to change the station or channel.

If you're asked, "Why should people read your book?"

Don't start with a statement like, "Well, there are a lot of people today who find they're living in families with two incomes, and the issue of the family car becomes very important . . ." You've just lost them out there! Who cares? Whatever you're going to say after a start like *that* is meaningless. They've forgotten the question. Try something like, "Every person in the United States between the ages of 24 and 69 has had [this experience]. My book explains what it's all about and how to deal with it." Knock them over in two sentences and then go into more detail as time allows with the next most interesting thing and then the next on down the line.

Nearly everyone is frightened when first going on television or radio. You feel nervous, vulnerable, anxious and inadequate. The possibility of making a fool of yourself is a more powerful fear than the fear of death itself with some people. Lacking experience, you seem to feel that you'll be struck stupid or faint when the first hint of criticism is aimed at you, or in some inexplicable way, just lose control altogether.

All you're really doing is having a simple conversation about your favorite subject with just one person. Look right into his or her eyes and ignore all distractions, just like when you pay attention to a friend in normal conversation. The camera, or the microphone, is a piece of inanimate furniture. Forget it! Force it out of your mind. Pretend it's not there. Instead, memorize the following "mantra." Focus your mind on this pleasant thought and keep repeating it to yourself—"I am the *best* possible person to talk about this subject; this is the *best* possible opportunity for me to talk about it; I *love* doing what I'm doing." The more often you say it, the better you'll feel and the more your fears will subside as you say it, mean it and *believe* it throughout the course of the interview. You *do* deserve credit for writing your book and you *have* become an expert on the subject. You

wouldn't have been prompted to write it and then suc-
ceeded in getting it published if you weren't qualified.
Accept the honors and the privileges that go with this
higher calling.

You have to realize what a privilege it is to be interviewed and be positive about yourself. This represents
the beginning of the confidence that is so necessary for
sales effectiveness. Once you do, you'll begin to see this
interview not as something you have to suffer through,
but as a pleasant experience. It will cease to be some
draconian obstacle course created to torture you. It will
turn instead into a wonderful chance to share something
you care about passionately, something you're uniquely
qualified to talk about. It should actually start to be *fun*.

When your big moment comes, be sure to dress the
part. Navy is the best color for both men and women.
Avoid stripes and prints. A good rule of thumb is to
wear what television news anchors wear. You might
want to ask your contact person if their staff will do
your makeup.

Additional notes:
Above all, BE COMFORTABLE AND BE YOURSELF.
You are the one in charge of the interview.

Remember that TV FLATTENS THE EMOTIONS, so add
a little energy and smile appropriately. Sit forward in your
chair to show you are engaged in the conversation. Don't
clasp your hands. It produces tension and limits your
ability to gesture.

ANTICIPATE the typical questions. Ask yourself, "What
type of show is this?" and "What is the ability of the interviewer?" Be prepared to respond to the questions with
short, simple and to-the-point answers...but not with just
blunt, one-word answers like "yes" or "no" or "right," which

can get very boring.

VISUALIZE YOUR AUDIENCE and talk to that audience *through* your interviewer.

USE QUOTABLE LANGUAGE. Put yourself in the reporter's shoes. He/she is trying to get a good story in a short time. Think in terms of "soundbites"—short, pointed and colorful quotes in which the message is clear.

AVOID COMPLICATED LANGUAGE, i.e., words that could be foreign to the general public. If your book deals with psychology, for example, the use of technical or professional terminololgy such as unipolar, bipolar, psychosocial, psychopharmacology, or co-morbidity may shut out your audience.

REPEAT MAIN POINTS. "Three's a charm" when being interviewed. Work your message in three times during the course of the interview. At least one of them will survive the cutting room floor.

USE STATISTICS AND FIGURES. They bring home the reality of what you're saying, but don't overdo it.

USE REAL-LIFE EXAMPLES of people who illustrate the message of your book.

RESPOND WITH POSITIVE COMMENTS even if the questions may stimulate a negative or defensive answer. Examples...

Q. What about [pharmaceutical brand name]? Aren't all anti-depressants potentially dangerous?

A. Antidepressants have been approved by the Federal

Drug Administration for many years. They've helped many, many people to overcome the symptoms of clinical depression.

OR . . .

Q. Aren't the pharmaceutical manufacturers and the psychiatrists going to make a fortune from the sale of the drugs you advocate?

A. We're delighted to have the financial support that makes it possible to educate millions about depression, a very treatable illness.

Hold the thought that this is going to be *your* day. You're going to impress the host and the audience with your command of the situation. If you're not convinced yet, then get the "success experiences" you need right now with local clubs and organizations that will let you make speeches.

CHAPTER SIX

Phon-er
or
Phon-ey

—Chapter Six—
A practiced, well-developed telephone
manner...patient and yet persistent...
will help to get your message across.

STEPS SIXTEEN THROUGH EIGHTEEN

Prior to printing . . .

16. Prepare pre-publication announcement ads

17. Send announcement to key buyers

18. Phone call follow-up to media

Step 16. Prepare pre-publication announcement ads—
If you don't have the budget to advertise in the New York
Times, get in touch with business, community or service
groups that publish directories and newsletters (see Gray
Pages section in the back of this book). Most of them have
very low advertising rates. If their membership matches
your target audience, find out the exact requirements of
the publication. Don't neglect the offbeat. Programs for
charity events, the local symphony or religious publications might be just the ticket.

You should try to attract the prospective reader in the
ad's headline. Use words that push their "hot button" and
make a book buyer stop and read. Include what the book is

about and how to order it. Include a clip-out coupon for easy ordering. Be direct and clear. For more information on how to phrase your ad, pick up one of the standard books on advertising writing by David Ogilvy or John Caples, or call Gaughen Public Relations at (805) 965-8482 for a free copy of *Advertising That Sells.*

Step 17. Send out announcements to key buyers— They are the people who make decisions for distributors. You'll find them listed in the *Literary Market Place.* Make it a simple, one-page letter explaining what your book is about, who your readers will be and why they will want to purchase your book. Include a "bounce-back" return postcard as in Step #8.

Step 18. Follow-up with a phone call to the media as you send out news releases— Each time you do something newsworthy (including those speeches to community groups), send out a release. In your phone call you'll want to ask if there's anything else the reporter or editor needs to know, if they want to send someone to cover the event, or if there's any way to make your releases more interesting to them.

TIP: Always ask media people if they are on deadline before you start to talk. If they're in a hurry, ask when it would be a good time to call back.

TELEPHONE TIPS
On average, you have approximately 10-20 seconds to interest an editor or show producer in your story. Be prepared before you pick up the phone. Have all of the information about your book in front of you (names, addresses, press run, etc.) It's your job to suggest specific story lines. Once you've gotten their attention, make their job as easy as possible. If you can provide names and

phone numbers of people they may want to interview about your book, tell them (see Steps 18 and 56).

Be sure you . . .

1. Always follow up. When you make a contact by phone, follow it up with a letter restating what you spoke about and provide any information you promised. If you don't follow up, nothing will happen!

2. Get someone to help you if you aren't very good on the phone. This doesn't necessarily mean you have to get a publicist. Tap a friend, relative, or anyone who has a phone.

3. Use a press release and follow it up. Call and make sure it got to the right person.

4. Always keep your database updated. Editors and producers move around a great deal. It does no good to send your press kit (cover letter, news release, author photo, book cover, etc.) to someone who no longer works for the station or magazine. Use your phone to find out.

5. Keep good notes. Follow up each contact made with a letter. Keep notes of your conversations with that person on a copy of the letter.

6. Keep your Rolodex updated. Whenever you start a new book promotion, go through your Rolodex and pull out the cards for the publications you want to approach (*Time, People*, etc.). Use it as a way to generate ideas.

7. Do your research. Go to the library or your local bookstore and look through some of the publications you want to approach. This will familiarize you with the publication and its focus.

8. Even if you're frustrated because you can't get through to the person you're trying to call, don't use rude language with a secretary or receptionist! Be positive, no matter what *they* say. These people have a job to do. One of their duties is to protect their employer from pesky phone calls. Respect their position, ask for their opinion on how best to approach their employer. In general, you'll get some good, inside advice.

9. Persist, but don't be a pest. If you hear in their voice they are busy, ask if you might call back in a week or so. They will appreciate your sensitivity, and it will give you permission to contact them again with your suggestion.

10. Don't lie. You are developing contacts with the press every time you talk to someone. If they can't trust you, they won't help you.

11. Don't avoid going after the big publications. It's always worth a try. They need news just as much as the smaller ones and they take no more effort than an article in your local newspaper.

12. Don't give up, even if you feel like it. Just remember, it has been estimated that over 70 percent of all news has been placed in the various media by someone like yourself.

13. Don't mention other competing publications that have written about your book. Many editors will not run a story if it has already appeared in a competitor's publication. If asked, tell the truth, but don't volunteer the information.

Remember: The press feeds on itself. An article in a trade or professional journal will allow you to pursue articles in non-competing publications, such as general interest magazines, consumer magazines, newspapers, newsletters, and other larger national publications, as well as appearances on television and radio.

CASE HISTORY: *Antennas Up...Keep Looking!*

Ruth Klein is president of The Marketing Source, a public relations and marketing firm. She holds a masters degree in psychology and is a member of the National Speaker's Association. She is the author of the book *Where Did The Time Go? A Working Woman's Guide to Creative Time Management* and has been interviewed on national radio and television stations such as CNBC and in the print media (*New York Daily News, First For Women* magazine and others). She conducts seminars on How to Make Time to Market Yourself, Time Management and Communication Skills.

As a publicist for authors as well as an author herself, she has found a number of effective ways to sell books other than just in bookstores.

• Identify groups of people who could use your book. "My book *Where Did The Time Go?* for example, is especially directed toward female college students, therapists who specialize in women's issues (for themselves as well as their clients), gift buyers, customers of beauty salons, employees and clients of temporary placement agencies, and other female-oriented locations or groups," Klein said.

• Keep your antenna up at all times. If you stay focused on selling your book, your subconscious will take over and keep a "look-out" for you. "Once, when I was driving on the freeway," Klein said, "I noticed a diaper service truck . . . BINGO! New moms would love to receive a few timely tips on managing their time and their lives more effectively. Since I figured there are hundreds of diaper services nationally, I began contacting them by phone and mail and proposing the idea of using my book as a premium, a 'give-away' that could generate business for them."

• Promote your book as a business-to-customer or person-to-person "Thank You" gift. Businesses are always looking for ways to show their clients they appreciate their patronage. Parents are also looking for ways to thank their children's teachers or coaches. Klein remembers, "One mother bought six of my books to give to all of her daughter's female teachers."

• Stay visible. You may have written the best, most informative, suspenseful and enjoyable book, but if people don't know about it, it simply won't sell. So send a press release about your book to newspapers and magazines, and/or write an article for your local newspapers related to your book's theme and make sure your credentials and your book's title get prominently mentioned. Have friends organize book-signing parties for you either in their homes or, even better, in a public location, and announce each party with a press release inviting the public. Call local organizations that relate to your theme (women's clubs and associations in the case of Klein's book) and let them know how available and entertaining you are as a speaker. Offer to speak for free if they will send a press release to the newspapers in their area with your picture.

Join one highly-visible organization that best represents your subject and stay active.

• Pitch ideas to contributing writers of newspapers and magazines, especially those you frequently read. Their editors are constantly in need of articles on interesting topics like yours. Remember to be helpful—find interesting "slants" to your book's theme, even news events that relate to your subject, and turn them into article ideas that mention your book's title.

• Contact radio stations. There are hundreds of stations that welcome and encourage telephone interviews with authors. Call them first, send them your press kit material, then call them again to make sure that they've received it. This gives you several chances to sell them on the idea. Then arrange for a time they'd like to interview you on the air. With every success of this kind, each following contact becomes easier. You're more at ease, and they're more impressed with the exposure and interest you've already generated.

"Years of experience have shown me that an author can push sales to a profitable, even a best-selling level, if this kind of effort is put forth," said Klein.

CHAPTER SEVEN

Target Practice... for Real!

—Chapter Seven—
It's time to zero in on some big
game: Wholesalers, both large
and small, as well as the very
lucrative non-traditional markets.

STEPS NINETEEN THROUGH TWENTY-FIVE

Prior to printing . . .

19. *Review (and adjust) your strategic plan*

20. *Run pre-publication ads*

21. *Mail pre-publication offer to targeted organization audience*

22. *Plan non-traditional promotional programs*

23. *Contact larger book wholesalers/distributors*

24. *Follow-up on larger wholesalers with mailing*

25. *Mail brochure/flyer to smaller wholesalers*

Step 19. Review (and adjust) your strategic plan—
You've learned a lot from all your calls and research. It's time to reflect and refocus your marketing plan to position your book to be in the path of your buyer at least *seven* effective times. Your sales results will be based on how well you convince them they need your book and why.

Step 20. Run pre-publication ads—
It's nice to have money on hand from the sale of your book before it is even published. Well-planned and well-placed pre-publication ads are one source for pre-orders. Select magazines, journals or other media with your readers in mind. Choose only those that match your readers' profile and work out a system to track the results with several different placements (i.e., a different phone number or extension on each), continuing with only the ones that are bringing in the best results.

Tom and Marilyn Ross, who own About Books, Inc. of Buena Vista, Colorado, suggest guarantees as one answer to increasing book sales. Offering a guarantee in your ad relieves apprehension on the part of potential buyers. It tells them if they're dissatisfied they do have a recourse. Interestingly enough, if you've created a sound product, very few people will take advantage of this.

There are many kinds of guarantees, all the way from seven days to a lifetime in length. Statistics show the longer the guarantee, the *less* likely you are to have returns. Consumers somehow figure there is no urgency in returning the merchandise and keep putting it off. Ultimately, they forget. And so, even though it may sound like a ludicrous thing to do, a lifetime guarantee is often more effective and trouble-free than a 30-day guarantee, since you're less likely to be refunding any money.

Besides guaranteeing your product, reassure purchasers in other ways.

For instance, guarantee delivery of the replacement or substitute book within 48 hours, or, in the case of audio tapes, guarantee an equally prompt replacement of a defective tape.

Guarantees are particularly important when running small classified ads which ask directly for the sale. In today's economy—where ads in major magazines can cost anywhere from $5 to $7 per word—you need to say a lot with few words to be cost-effective. By printing "satisfaction guaranteed" or "money-back guarantee" in the ad, you can reassure your potential customers.

"When we write promotional literature for a direct-mail campaign," says Marilyn Ross, "we always put the guarantee in a fancy box and personally sign it. This focuses attention on this important aspect of the offer."

So, when you are looking for another way to increase book sales, remember guarantees alleviate the buyer's concerns. The fact that you stand behind your merchandise reassures those who might be apprehensive. It's a subtle way of helping your potential buyer make a decision.

If you don't know the first thing about adverising, you'll be glad to hear that successful self-publisher Dan Poynter advises authors not to spend money on display ads. "Instead send out 400 books and press kits for review to the media that reaches your target audience," he says. "Figure shipping cost at $2.50 each, then multiply that times 400 and you get $1000.00. Where can you get decent ad space for $1000.00, space that would do as good a job as the real thing?" he asks.

Poynter then counsels authors to "follow-up month after month with a news release about how your book solves problems. And always include order information," he emphasizes. This approach, combined with direct marketing to his target audience, has brought Poynter years of success for the books he's written on his specialty, the sport of parachuting. Persistence like this could work for you too.

Step 21. Mail pre-publication offer to targeted organizations/audience—

There is no faster, cheaper or easier way to test results than with a direct letter and a tear-off form or bounce-back (return) postcard for orders. You can sell the benefits of reading your book better this way than in any magazine ad or radio or TV spot. Also, you can follow-up with a phone call and record the reader's response to your letter and offer. When your book is finished, you're then prepared to create the perfect sales letter from all this input. Think about including a price for volume sales or a special offer with a time limit and remind everyone you are also available for speaking engagements.

CASE STUDY: *Ideas Right Under Your Nose*

A book idea can actually start with a targeted organization. Author Jane Kurtz of Grand Forks, North Dakota, who's written three historical activity books, was talking with a fellow writer whose mother had spent years as the executive director of a museum in Trinidad, Colorado. "She said her mother had told her that families would come through the museum bookstore," Kurtz recalled, "looking for local history written for children and they wouldn't find any.

"Having said that, we looked at each other (otherwise known as market research) and *Bingo!* our publishing company, Roots and Wings, was born."

Of course, they had no money. Do any writers? So they called on the local Trinidad Historical Society and proposed to co-venture an historical activity book about Trinidad, Colorado. The society bought it. Literally. In the check they received, the authors had included a modest fee for themselves and, in return for the investment, they offered to turn over most of the proceeds for the book to the society. Then they set out to learn about printing books. They read books on self-publishing, talked to friends and bought books that were similar to what they had in mind.

"Our little company went on to publish other activity books on regional history and on the

Santa Fe and Oregon trails. None made us rich. All made us some money. And with none did we invest our own capital—because we never had any," Kurtz said.

"Three years after we plunged into the publishing business, my first picture book was accepted by Albert Whitman. In 1990, Macmillan published my children's non-fiction book on Ethiopia. This year, Simon & Schuster will publish two picture books, and a third will be published by Houghton Mifflin. The *Oregon Trail* activity book has just been scheduled for its second printing and is selling very well in museums and gift shops.

"I would like to think publishers will invest ever greater amounts of money in my work," Kurtz commented. "But, in the meantime, I've never regretted the hours I've invested in my own publishing business."

Step 22. Plan non-traditional promotion programs— Think of how to get your book in front of your target audience. The Book Industry Study Group released figures in 1988 showing that one out of every four books purchased by consumers is bought at a non-book store presentation or retail outlet.

Try approaching grocery, variety, hobby, gift, liquor, discount and camera stores, or even a car wash cashier's office, etc. Find the manager and ask a lot of questions. Who are their customers? How does the management make buying decisions? What trends are they aware of? Ask if they will stock your book, even on consignment. Millions of dollars worth of books are sold every year in this manner. Look for ingenious links between your book and other businesses, professions, institutions, organizations or individuals.

Be clever. Don't hold back! Even Club Med has sent authors on trips to promote books (all expenses paid) when the book proved to be of benefit to the typical Club Med traveler.

The same basic procedures can be followed as you . . .

Step 23. Contact large book wholesalers— Wholesalers are often willing to place your book in their catalogs and microfiche. Since they don't demand exclusivity, you can work with many of them for maximum exposure. They can be found listed in the *Literary Market Place* and in the Gray Pages section of this book. Bookstores like to purchase their books from wholesalers because they get quick delivery. The bookstore people know who they're dealing with, they know the number by heart, and they can always get in contact with them immediately. You'll get larger orders and have less paperwork if you deal with a large wholesaler. Think of them as your shipping department and as order takers for your book.

Wholesalers range from large, national firms to those who focus on small, special subject areas. Upon first contact, request a "Vendor Profile Questionnaire" and ask if they have other information or guidelines that would be helpful. Ask further about the discounts they require, their terms, the trade shows they attend, how they reach their markets and if they have a catalog.

Step 24. Follow-up on large wholesalers with a mailing— Be sure to fill out each wholesaler's form individually to meet their specific requirements. Be respectful of the format they have created. You can send your forms out all at once because wholesalers do not expect exclusivity on the distribution of your book. So don't stop when you've been accepted by one of them.

An excellent one-stop-shopping source for new book

information forms is:
   Book Marketing Made Easy
   by John Kremer
   51 North 5th Street
   Fairfield, IA 52556
   Phone: (515) 472-6130
   Fax: (515) 472-3186

Step 25. Mail brochure/flyer to smaller wholesalers—
When you do, request their specific forms and guidelines
and follow-up as in Step 24. Continue to follow-up, follow-
up and follow-up again with phone calls and post cards
telling them why there is such a demand for your book.

CHAPTER EIGHT

Be Shelf Conscious

—Chapter Eight—
Time to explore your partnership
with bookstore owners
for your mutual benefit.

STEPS TWENTY-SIX THROUGH THIRTY

Prior to printing . . .

26. Mail brochures/flyers to major bookstore chains

27. Phone follow-up to bookstore chains

28. Conduct mailing to independent bookstores

29. Send targeted mailing to specialized bookstores

30. Participate in co-op bookstore mailings

Step 26. Mail brochures/flyers to major bookstore chains—

You can make your own sales to major chain stores. Just be aware this is not always easy because they want to make sure your book fills their mass market need. Start with a phone call to Barnes & Noble, Waldenbooks, Crown, etc. and ask for the name of the appropriate buyer. Then, on a regular schedule, send that person information about your book.

Mail your brochures or flyers to as many book buyers

as your budget will allow (see Gray Pages section). Even better, meet with them in person. Clarrissa Pinkola Estes, author of *Women Who Run With the Wolves*, got her book on the best seller list in part because she spent an entire summer talking with buyers and booksellers. According to one newspaper reporter, the sales reps were transfixed by that first meeting and gave it their best. The independent and the chain booksellers featured her book prominently in their stores.

"Distributors and retailers love to help those who are willing and able to help themselves," states Aaron Silverman of SCB Distributors. "Don't assume for a minute that someone else will do your marketing for you, or do it better. Your personal participation in the selling process is important. If you only intend to write one book, you ought to have plenty of time to market it yourself. If you ever intend to write another one, all the more reason to make the first one a big success.

"The author is usually the best one to sell his own ideas," he maintains. "Personal visits to bookstores, participating in their promotions (book signing appearances) and meeting people at book conventions keeps you in close contact with your public, not to mention with others in the industry who could prove to be very helpful."

Step 27. Make follow-up calls to the bookstore chains on your mailing list—
Get in the habit of setting aside a couple of hours a day with a specific goal of 20 calls. If you're having a good day, keep calling. If it's a bad day, you'll know it. Give yourself permission to work on something that gives you more positive feedback, or just go out and take a walk for a while. With a carefully thought out presentation, a little time and a lot of practice, you should get very good on the phone. With a 30-second "benefit introduction" you should be able to get into a relaxed, mutually beneficial conversation. As a

writer you should be able to put more creativity into it than the average telemarketer.

In an interview once, the late legendary movie heart-throb Cary Grant confessed that he often had a problem whenever he tried to place a call. The secretary would ask him who he was, he would tell her, and she would faint. Assuming you haven't got this problem, once you get in a comfortable daily habit of placing your calls it should go very well.

Harvey McKay, of *Swim With The Sharks Without Being Eaten Alive* fame, used a phone call to Crown Books to inform them of the orders for his book by other chain bookstores. This single phone call resulted in an order of 5,000 books. There are over 200 bookstore chains, so don't give up.

Step 28. Conduct a mailing to independent bookstores—

After the mailing, do the same telephone routine as you did with the chain stores. If you have the time and you're short on funds, map out the local circuit of bookstores listed in your telephone company's Yellow Pages and travel around. Go into the store, shake the owner's hand and identify yourself as a local author. Independent bookstore owners have a love of the written word and an empathy for writers that most chainstore employees can't match.

ADVICE FROM AN INDEPENDENT BOOKSTORE OWNER

Barry Martin is the co-owner of BOOK'em Mysteries, a specialty bookstore in South Pasadena, California.

His advice to authors: "Build your local constituency. Call up and let your neighborhood booksellers know you are a local author and you have a new book coming out. Then get to know the owner, the manager, the employees and their customers personally."

Build Editorial Constituency

"Authors can build an *editorial* constituency," he suggests. "One of the most successful is Susan Conant, a writer who specializes in dog-lover mysteries. She constantly writes feature articles for regional and national dog-owner and veterinary publications. These persistent journalistic efforts have greatly increased her following. In 1990, her paperback sales were modest. Today she has people standing in line to buy her newest novel in hard cover.

"Author, Rebecca Rothenburg, whose specialty is botanical mysteries, succeeds by continually writing articles for national botanical publications and speaking before botanical societies throughout the region, and beyond. She knows we stock her book, so she sends all of her friends and acquaintances here. I believe we've sold well over a hundred of her books," notes Martin.

"People like Rothenburg profit from this arrangement by guaranteeing themselves a larger royalty check. Rothenburg insures more books are sold and fewer are returned.

"As most professional writers understand, publishers are only going to deal with their 'A-List' people. If you're a mid-list author, the responsibility really falls on you to do the majority of your promotion," Martin emphasizes. "The dollars just aren't there for you to travel. Corporate decisions are made every day as to which author gets the limited publicity dollars for advertising, tours and book signings. They decide which authors are going to be pushed editorially and which books are going to be submitted for review," Martin states.

The Bookstore Partnership

"Just because a book is published doesn't mean it's going to sell," Martin warns. "Well-written books can just stay on the shelf and never move. If at all possible, we believe in being in partnership with the author. If we can get a galley proof of their new book and read it even before it comes out, we can 'hand sell' it by recommending it in advance of publication to every customer who comes in. 'Here's one you ought to consider. It's being released next month,' comes easily to mind when the storekeeper knows the author, the book and when it's coming.

"And," Martin states, "if we're friends with the author, it works the other way too. The author can say, 'I know they'll have a supply of my latest book over at BOOK'em Mysteries in South Pasadena.'"

Independent specialty bookstores have one great advantage over chain-store outlets. Their staff know their inventory and can recommend books. Larger operations move lots of books at discount, however their sales staff is often too uninformed or too busy to help.

"At specialty bookstores such as ours, we know exactly where everything is, how many books are left of each title and often what each book is about," Martin says. "Consequently, independent specialty bookstores, in my opinion, are the best places for a first-time author to start building a following. Throughout any large city, there are many diverse areas and specialties—children's books, aviation books, mystery books, romance, science fiction, etc. These store managers and owners are eager to foster mutually profitable relationships with new authors.

"Sue Grafton, Elizabeth George and many other top writers have started in this manner," Martin adds. "We feel a strong responsibility to stock a local author, even if other bookstores don't. We try even harder if the author is from our region."

Book Review Publications

"Since the retailer hasn't time to read every book that comes along," Martin says, "it's important to get reviewed in the best book review publications, such as; *The New York Times Book Review, The Washington Post, The New*

York Review of Books, Publishers Weekly, and *Booklist* (for the libraries). We all read these critiques on a regular basis and generally accept what they say about the book.

"If authors will 'mine' their hometown area first, and take advantage of the store's advertising budget and exposure to its customers, their following will eventually spread," Martin says reassuringly. "This is exactly how novice writers can climb the ladder to their publisher's mid-list, even to the A-list, if they persevere."

Step 29. Do a target mailing to specialty stores— Research shows that less than 35% of the population of the United States has ever been in a bookstore. Then, how do you get your books in front of the rest of the people? Retail outlets are the answer. Look for specialized retailers that suit your topic such as supermarkets, drug stores, toy stores, travel agencies, inspirational/religious stores, gardening or home improvement centers, sporting goods stores, or especially-for-women stores. Museum gift shops are good places to consider if your book is especially attractive. Try hospital gift stores for inspirational material and quick, easy-to-read subjects.

Learn everything you can about these retail outlets. There are great differences in operational procedures and discounts. Begin your research by attending trade shows catering to that specialty, read the magazines in that field and ask a lot of questions.

Since mailings are more likely to be cost-effective when they contain several items, make a list of compatible items and include them in your order form along with your book. Try brainstorming with a group of associates and collect ideas such as an audiotaped version of your book; other books on the same subject purchased wholesale in limited quantities; T-shirts emblazoned with your book's cover design in full-color; posters complementing your book's subject, such as a photo of a popular baseball player if your subject is baseball or a floral painting if you're dealing with gardening. Make as many as 5 to 20 follow-up calls, even if it's to the same person. It may result in a substantial order.

Step 30. Participate in co-op bookstore mailings— Many large chains and independent book stores do their own book review mail order brochures. Ask the manager or owner if your book might be considered for inclusion in their next printing.

Take a look at your calendar for the next three months. Plot where you'll be and arrange meetings there with book buyers (and even for book signings) now. No matter where you travel, or for what reason, allow time in your schedule for visits to local bookstores.

We suggest that you work up a basic form letter explaining what you have to offer and that you'll be in town on a certain date. Always send a (bounce back) reply card with your letter so they can check off the possibilities they would like to pursue.

On the next page is a sample bounce-back card listing the several statements recommended for the bookstore proprietor to check off.

An added *plus:* you are now making business trips, which means at least part of your expenses may be deductible.

TIP: If you have been lax in keeping track of your expenses, start now to change your habits. As well as travel expenses, every telephone, postage or duplicating cost may be a deductible expense. You could be throwing away a small fortune over several months. Don't short-change yourself just because you think it's tedious to keep records. If necessary, find an organized person and have him or her show you a simple method for doing it.

REVIEW BOOK REQUEST

I would like to receive a review/examination copy of:

Book title: _____

Name of publication or broadcast station: _____

Name of reviewer: _____

Full job title: _____

Mailing address: _____

Circulation: _____ Frequency: _____ Ave. no of pages: _____

Brief description of publication: _____

_____

Audience profile: _____

Comments (optional): _____

_____

CASE STUDY: *Remain Calm, Smile and Forge Ahead!*

"A lot of writers are solitary people," says author Tony Johnston. "They find it very hard to sell a book."

She suggests that the more you've been around your audience (in her case, children) the better. If you've been a parent, a scout leader, a teacher, or if you just happen to like kids, you may feel less anxious around them when promoting your book. "Of course," she admits, "becoming a parent to help you relax with your audience would be an extreme measure to take."

Johnston, the creator of over 60 colorful picture books, often makes the difficult transition from the quiet home where she lives and writes, to the chaotic world of airline travel, book conventions, the classroom, the auditorium, or the bookstore—wherever her readers may live or learn.

She's always learning from these experiences. Recently, en route to a book signing at Stanford University, her plane never left the ground. Finally, when she did board another plane many hours later, her luggage did not. Unfortunately, the luggage contained her speech, and she had to scramble to rewrite it from scratch. As a result, she offers this piece of advice to traveling authors: *Always leave the day before your event* and *carry your essentials.*

"That way everyone can relax— author, bookstore owner and patrons—and you won't be in a lather when, and if, you arrive."

Johnston also reminds us that the unexpected can foil even the best laid plans. She advises, "Remain calm, poised and professional. Smile and forge ahead, or, in the worst case, grit your teeth and forge ahead.

"Once I was making a presentation in an elementary school gym full of five- to eleven-year-olds. Blessed with great peripheral vision, I soon noticed a boy off to one side moving closer and closer to me. What attracted him I'll never know," Johnston said. "But the result was...he threw up on me. *Remain calm, smile and forge ahead.* He was quickly ushered off by his teacher, and I proceeded with my talk.

"The unexpected can happen no matter how old your audience is," she warned.

"Once, while giving a talk to parents in Mexico City, I was leaning on the table, warming to my theme. A young man casually unzipped his black leather jacket, removed his pet iguana and let it stroll around the table. *Smile, forge ahead, remain calm*—and bring along your sense of humor.

"It's always a good idea to ask the person inviting you what kind of situation you can expect. This tends to minimize surprises and raise your comfort level. Still, someone throwing up or people with hidden iguanas really can't be planned for."

In another instance, while promoting her latest book, *The Cowboy and The Black-Eyed Pea,* from G.P. Putnam's Sons, she followed a dog who was autographing with its paw print.

"It was my hour to sign books for the people waiting in line," she explained. "When I neared the table with my publisher's representative, there sat the author who preceded me with the main character of his book in his lap, lifting its paw back and forth from ink pad to title page. My first reaction was, 'What are they trying to tell me?' *Remain calm, smile and forge ahead*." Johnston emphasized that when you are to appear at a bookstore or at a more non-traditional location (school, hobby shop, etc.) for a signing, be sure that your hosts take full responsibility for arranging advertising, mail-outs, posters, and stocking the location with your books. At least a week before, call the person in charge and finalize the plans for your visit. You may also want to request copies of their promotional pieces. If your audience hasn't been notified, you and your host could be the only two people attending.

How does Johnston handle her audience once she arrives? The audience generally consists of children and since she has three daughters, has taught 4th grade and likes children, she's comfortable and knows what to expect. "But if, as an author, you feel that confronting kids is like walking into a den of lions, it's probably a good idea to take your publisher's rep along to act as a 'buffer' between you and the 'lions,'" she advised.

Publicity people who send authors on tour need to know the abilities and limitations of their writers to help them prepare for their audiences.

Johnston added that special talents can help grab an audience and make a lasting impression. "Sid Fleischman is a magician. I've seen his magic tricks mesmerize his audiences. But even without tricks, kids love his books. He is a magician with words." One lesson Johnston has drawn from her experiences: *Make your presentation as visual as possible.*

"If you've written a story about a quilt, bring a quilt along," she suggests. "Or tape all the rough drafts of your book together and serpentine them around the room to illustrate the amazing amount of rewriting that goes into your work. Or, you might publicly weigh the rewrites. After seven years of working on the book, *Yonder*, I accumulated an impressive amount of poundage.

"Schools treat author visits differently. One school principal apparently had no idea I was coming, or forgot. She showed no interest in my being there," Johnston recalls. "I said to myself, *'Remain calm, smile and forge ahead,'* and I did.

"Most people are hospitable and *do* take full advantage of these educational opportunities. Holland Hall School in Tulsa, Oklahoma, recently welcomed me so warmly that I look forward to going back. I was met at the airport and, throughout my stay, treated like royalty," she says. "Both the children *and* their parents participated in the events. Everyone had read my books and had good, thoughtful questions to ask. And, from talking to the school librarian, I got an unexpected bonus, the idea for my book, *Walking Home.*

"One final thing, whether it's a bookseller, a school principal, the classroom teacher who did something special, someone who drove you some-where, or anyone who helped you with the event—write that person a thank you note the minute you get home. No—better yet—write it on the plane going home," Johnston concluded.

In non-traditional presentations, people will pay full price for your books. So, if your fee is covered, and you sell as many books as you can sign, your efforts can be well compensated.

Authors should use varying presentation styles and try to gain practice and exposure in front of friendly local audences before signing up for a tour or making more formal presentations.

Once your flyers are on their way to your specialty store contact people, those who can arrange book signings or speaking engagements, contact the rest of your "distri-bution team." If you have a trade publisher, ask for the names, addresses and phone numbers of their contact people at wholesalers, major book chains and indepen-dent bookstores. Let them and your publisher know exactly what you're doing to be actively involved in the follow-up phase of marketing your book.

CHAPTER NINE

Mingle Among 'Em

—Chapter Nine—
Book fairs, trade shows, the
American Booksellers Association
Convention, book clubs...all put you
face to face with your publishing
contemporaries and readers.

STEPS THIRTY-ONE THROUGH THIRTY-SEVEN

Prior to printing . . .

31. Advertise or list book in special magazine editions

32. Participate in book fairs and trade shows

33. Register with the ABA

34. Contact library distributors and wholesalers

35. Contact magazines about periodical rights for excerpts

36. Contact magazines about condensation rights

37. Contact book clubs

Step 31. Advertise or list in special magazine editions—
The subject of your book will determine the best magazines
to consider for paid advertising. Look for highly specialized
magazines that cater to a narrow audience rather than to
general interest magazines. To get a better match of readers' interests, request the magazine's editorial calendar
and learn what topics will be highlighted in the upcoming
editions.

Don't call the advertising department for a calendar. Send a SASE (self-addressed stamped envelope) to the editorial department. Write: "Please send editorial calendar" on the envelope.

Find out advertising costs before you create your ad. Ask if the magazine allows fulfillment or "per inquiry" ads. Like personal injury lawyers, these ads only cost you money if you win (sales, that is). Typically, the magazine takes one-third to one-half of the money sent in, leaving you the rest. Although this seems like a lot, it saves you money on the front end and lets you test a market with zero investment.

To learn the basics of successful advertising, read *How to Create and Evaluate Advertising that Sells* by Jim Alexander.

Step 32. Participate in book fairs and trade shows— Each month, book shows are held across the country. Some feature books of general interest. Others are very specific, such as the Society of Southwestern Authors or the Dog Writers' Association of American, Inc. Many can be found in *Literary Market Place*. The *AAP Directory* (Association of American Publishers) is a fine source for educational, library and associated subjects. They are also listed in writers magazines such as *Writer's Digest* and *The Writer*.

Participating in local book fairs can cost less than $100 and is an excellent way to meet readers and buyers for your book.

Exhibition space at major shows can easily cost in excess of $1000. That doesn't take into consideration the cost of travel, lodging, food, and the expense of creating a booth display and on-the-spot assembly. There *are* economic options. The American Library Association offers bargain rates to the small press publishers, and major associations sponsor regional or local book fairs.

Conventions and conferences of professional and business associations offer additional opportunities. Here you can sell books as well as meet your audience in the flesh.

Book fairs are the best place to get a crash course in the publishing industry and your place in it. We advise you to try it at least once.

The main sponsors of book fairs are:

•The American Booksellers Association
560 White Plains Road
Tarrytown, NY 10591
(914) 631-7800/Fax: (212) 631-8391
(800) 637-0037

•The American Library Association
50 East Huron Street
Chicago, IL 60611
(312) 944-6780/Fax: (312) 440-0901

•The National Association of College Stores
528 East Lorain Street
P.O. Box 58
Oberlin, OH 44074
(216) 776-7777

Step 33. Register with the ABA (American Bookseller Association)—

The ABA brings you information and resources as well as exhibit and marketing opportunities. Fortunately, you don't have to be a member to benefit from their outstanding services. For instance, the *ABA's Book Buyer's Handbook* lists pertinent facts about you as a self-publisher so that booksellers can find you and your book(s). Get an application form for your listing by writing to them at the address listed in Step 32.

CASE STUDY: *A Candid View of The ABA*

New writers can be easily awe struck by all the excitement, the semi-famous celebrities and the "big business" atmosphere of the ABA.

Editor and publisher Elisabeth Sifton sees the ABA as a strange tribal rite that takes place at the height of spring somewhere at the heart of the American culture. The following is an exerpt from the article she wrote in her magazine *The Nation:*

> "The ABA is a trade fair that pulls together tens of thousands of booksellers, publishers, book buyers, sales directors, rights managers, publicists, sales representatives and big-time executives.
>
> "The initial purpose of the ABA was to enable buyers from book shops nationwide to place orders for the next season's books with the publishers' salespeople. However, faxes, computers and other important changes in the business have made this serious and lively commercial activity somewhat obsolete.
>
> "Even though this is the case, publishers know they should stay close to writers and to booksellers. Indeed, great publishers always have, and still do. It is the only possible way to survive, since the known truth is that profit depends not just on the few big sellers of the current season but on the steady sales of older titles. The 'back-listed' books published during the past year provide a huge proportion of most publishers' income. Publishers must cultivate writers and readers for both kinds of books in their inventories.
>
> "There have never been so many good booksellers in our history—resourceful, socially active

and committed, well-read and good at business.
Many of them might in earlier times have been
ministers or teachers. They have an all but
evangelical fervor about increasing readership
and literacy. They believe that Americans can
and should read books. They truly care about
multiculturalism. They want the United States
to live up to its promises, and they are aston-
ished and pleased by the huge possibilities that
its culture offers to writers and readers. They
look at the horrifying statistics on the decline of
reading—more than half of American house-
holds in a given year may never purchase a
book—merely as indicators of what huge growth
potential their business has. There are all those
unconverted nonreaders to bring into the fold!
There's nowhere to go but up!

One couldn't have better colleagues than
these brave, shrewd independent booksellers,
who reinvented the idea of the well-stocked
cavernous bookstore which encourages browsing
and unexpected purchases, which presents books
as the physical and mental pleasure they are.
These business people, some of whom have
expanded their stores into mini-chains of their
own, are the people who learned from, challenged
and in some respects prevailed over the chains—
Walden, Dalton, Crown—that shortsighted
Cassandras claimed a decade ago would kill off
the independents. With equal savvy about inventory control and marketing strategy, but a sub-
tler, more responsible and community-based
sense of how to develop and expand the customer
pool, the independents soon forced the big chain
companies to copy them, which they are now
doing with their famous superstores.

Writers have been quick to appreciate that all this has changed the shape and nature of literary life in America. They happily accept invitations (worked out jointly between publisher and bookshop) to give readings and talks at the stores. They come to know the buyers, meet the retail purchasers, develop local audiences one by one across the country. These new encounters are mostly paid for by publishers, but were invented by booksellers.

None of this work could be done without the computerized technologies that make it feasible to control vast and complex inventories of hardcover, paperback, and old and new books.

In the noise of the ABA convention—where sensory overload taxes the body and wearies the soul—sensible, wise men and women can still be heard, doing honorable work as they did in the early years of the convention. The chances remain excellent that our intellectual and literary life will continue into the next century.

CASE STUDY: *An ABA Debriefing*
(from Marcus Meleton, a first time attendee)

Attending the ABA Convention as a first time author who had taken on the task of self-publishing was like being a kid in a candy store. It was difficult to keep my objectives in mind. There were give-aways galore and free book signings by authors you thought you would never meet. All participants of the book making process were there with book buyers circulating and the press spread throughout.

As mentioned, there was far too much for me to do. So, prior to my arrival, I listed my goals and prioritized them. What I did there was to focus my efforts towards my greatest needs. I used the rest as distractions when I needed a break.

My book had just been printed, so my first objective was to find a distributor. I marked all the distributors and wholesalers that were listed in the Program and Location Guide. On the first day of the convention, I began visiting them one by one. A month of telephoning would never have equaled what I was able to accomplish in just a few short days. I met with people face to face rather than by long distance. I could get a feel for those whose services most suited my needs and I could quickly eliminate those who didn't.

My next step was to ask other roving authors and representatives about their experiences with the companies I had visited. With those contacts I was able to get an additional list of prospects which I then put in order by preference.

I had been warned that many people will not collect books at the ABA because the convention practically rains books. The task of searching out distribution is therefore not done on the spot. I did follow-up book mailings and phone calls. As always, the three rules of success in publicity are follow-up, follow-up, follow-up. Other terms are pester, bother, and be a pain.

My next objective was obtaining press for my book, not only to get name recognition, but to assist in getting the attention of distributors. I left large stacks of press releases in the convention center press room on the first day. What I learned is that there is a massive turnover of material. It is constantly being moved, covered up by other authors' materials, and thrown away. At night it is all eliminated. By the second day I began to visit the press room every other hour, leaving a few covers and releases in different locations in the room and on the coffee tables. Those on the coffee tables were thrown away. But with a title such as mine, *Nice Guys Don't Get Laid*, it would always get noticed. Occasionally, I left a book. I never found one remaining there by my next visit, so I likely nabbed an interested journalist.

I would strike up conversations with those from the press when I noticed the press markings on their badges. I don't know how much that helped, but combined with my material in the press room and any future promotions, I hoped recognition of my book would finally begin to hit home with them. Repetition like this is valuable.

One result was an article featuring my book in the *Dallas Morning News* a week after the convention closed. Lucky for me, I have a friend in Dallas who noticed it in the paper. There may have been more articles. Most reporters won't notify an author of a pending article. I know my efforts were effective because several people commented that they had seen my material.

Although press and distribution were my main concerns, I did much more. I had many chances to meet authors and to learn from their experiences. I've been in contact with several who have similar books and were willing to share leads with me. One of these resulted in promoting my book as a talk show subject.

As much as I enjoyed pushing my book, there was always time for fun. One was the Remainders' party, a group of writers with musical backgrounds who performed a rock concert for the ABA show. There, as with other parties, I was constantly meeting new people with shared interests.

Four days effort at the ABA equals a month of

phoning. Go there with your objectives clearly in mind, be ready to push your book, and follow-up, follow-up...*always* follow-up.

(Below is an article from the National Examiner, July 20, 1993)

Nice guys do finish last!

That's the message from the much-dumped Marcus Meleton Jr. — a single sweetheart who says he's too nice to get the girl.

"Women like to go off with the jerks and leave the nice guys behind with only wilted flowers and broken dreams," says the handsome 37-year-old engineer from Costa Mesa, California.

"The fact came home to me loud and clear one night.

"I went to a party where a drunken idiot began booming abuse at his girlfriend and the hostess. As he left, he made some crude remarks to another man's date and a fight broke out.

NICE GUYS never get the girls

"After it was over, he was escorted to the hospital by several of the best-looking women at the party, while the rest of us were left behind in the ruins."

Marcus was so shaken by the jerk vs. nice guy phenomenon that he wrote a book called Nice Guys Don't Get ---- (Sharkbait Press, Costa Mesa, CA).

"Every time a man is told he's a nice guy by a woman, he knows he's about to get dropped," says Marcus, who's never been married.

Now he's warning nice guys everywhere of what these rat-loving gals are telling them.

Here's what they say —

WHY WOMEN PREFER JERKS

and what they REALLY mean:

● You are so understanding. — You are easy to turn down.

● Maybe some other time. — If I don't have anything better to do.

● You say the nicest things. — You say all the things I wish a real boyfriend would say.

● What a nice guy. — You are a leper.

● I feel comfortable with you. — We're like brother and sister.

● You are such a good companion. — So is my dog Rover.

● I trust you. — You're boring. Why don't you lie to me?

● You're such a gentleman. — I like to use you.

He has a warning for women, too: "If a man doesn't treat you well now, it will only get worse!"

— *GWEN CARDEN*

Step 34. Contact library distributors and wholesalers—

Libraries—whether we are talking about public, private, school, or government—are the second largest source of book orders in the nation, right behind the retail book-sellers. Even in tough times, they spend almost one-and-a-half billion dollars a year on books. Predictably they purchase a lot of children's books and best sellers, but they also look to cover a wide range of topics to please the reading public.

TIP: In 1993, a new Yellow Pages directory for libraries was published. 30,000 libraries receive this directory free. This could be an excellent place for an ad:

> *The Librarian's Yellow Pages*
> *P.O. Box 179*
> *Larchmont , NY 10538*
> *(914) 834-7070/Fax: (914) 834-3053*
> *(800) 235-9723*

Libraries order through general wholesalers like Baker & Taylor, but also through two distributors: Quality Books and Unique Books. Both of them use sales representatives to sell books to libraries. Make sure these distributors are notified about your book in its early stages. That's how they get ahead of the whole-salers when it comes to orders.

Keep in mind the height and width of library shelves before you go to print. Otherwise you could be out of the running for library purchases. Strong selling points, besides a hot topic, are durable binding, a spine that displays the title clearly, and a standard shape (not oversized or undersized). A spiral binding will eliminate all possibilities for orders, and so will books with tests or questions that ask a reader to fill in the blanks.

Quality Books welcomes well-written self-published books, especially in fields that aren't crowded with material. They'll be glad to send you a New Book Information form and a sample of a Distribution to Libraries Agreement if you write to:

Quality Books, Inc.
918 Sherwood Drive
Lake Bluff, IL 60044-2204
(708) 295-2010/Fax: (708) 295-1556

Unique Books
4200 Grove Avenue
Gurnee, IL 60031
(708) 623-9171/Fax: (708) 623-7238

Step 35. Contact magazines about periodical rights for excerpts—
This can be a big money field, so competition is stiff. Major publications are inundated with requests, so consider smaller niche publications that are less likely to be overwhelmed.

If you are a novice at magazine writing, read about "Rights and the Writer" in any edition of the *Writers Market* before submitting your inquiry.

You don't have to send out your inquiries one-by-one. You can send out several at once as long as you don't send the same part or chapter to more than one editor at a time.

Send your news release, flyer and a query letter that explains how your material matches the interest of their reader. Include a couple of pages of the chapter you want to sell and a SASE (self-addressed stamped envelope). Give editors everything they need to make a decision.

Don't be afraid to follow up in a couple of weeks. After all, your publication clock is ticking. Get on the phone and find out what is happening. If you're going to be rejected, the sooner you know about it, the sooner you can change your presentation or pitch and contact another publication with a similar audience.

Step 36. Contact magazines about condensation rights—

Magazine excerpts or condensations are not only a source of increased income, they also expose potential purchasers (including bookstore owners) to your work.

There's a magazine for every person and for every topic. The selection at your local supermarket is just the tip of the iceberg. There are specialized publications on subjects from architecture to zoology. Somewhere in between you're bound to find several that match the contents of your book.

You probably have the primary research tool at hand to start your search of possible buyers: the annual *Writers Market*. Other excellent books are *Book Marketing Opportunities: A Directory* or the *Literary Market Place*.

Step 37. Contact book clubs—

Extra income and promotional exposure can come from book club sales. Book club people can be contacted at any phase of your book's life cycle from manuscript to publication. If you send your work in manuscript or galley form, just be sure to include cover art, your book flyer, publication date and price. This is an excellent time to talk the book club into joining in your print run, which means a bigger run (less cost per book) and enough income to pay for a substantial part of your printing bill.

Multiple submissions are acceptable. While the big clubs expect you to sell to them and no one else, the smaller ones don't (even if that's what they ask you to do).

You'll find book clubs listed in the *Literary Market*

Place and *Book Marketing Opportunities: A Directory.* Check each one carefully, especially those that target the smaller niche markets. Write for guidelines where offered and follow them closely.

Book club deals demand and expect negotiation skills. Don't be so excited about making a sale that you act like an over-eager first-time author, even if you are. If they tell you their policy is to pay in 90 days, ask for 30. If cash flow is important, consider offering a discount for even quicker payment.

NOTE: It's not too late to contact book clubs a month or so after your book is printed. If you've missed the opportunity prior to publication, the smaller book clubs are the place to go. If the material is relevant, some have been known to even reprint books of special interest to their readers.

CHAPTER TEN

This Could Make You a Fortune, Cookie

—Chapter Ten—
The foreign publishing and
specialty bookstore market
is a rich smorgasbord valued
in billions and billions
of American dollars.

STEPS THIRTY-EIGHT THROUGH FORTY-ONE

Prior to printing . . .

38. Contact foreign book publishers

39. Brainstorm non-traditional markets

40. Research and develop list of specialty book stores

41. Mail brochures/flyers to targeted specialty stores

Step 38. Contact foreign book publishers—

The *Literary Market Place* and *International Literary Market Place* lists foreign publishers with U.S. offices, U.S. agents of foreign publishers, and export representatives which means you don't have to go overseas to break into the lucrative international market.

How lucrative is it? U.S. authors export over nine hundred million dollars in book sales each year. Most are scientific, technical or professional titles, but bright ideas, how-tos and self-help books can easily cross boundaries as well. Many go to English-speaking countries like Canada, Great Britain and Australia. Other big buyers include

Japan, the Netherlands and West Germany.

Foreign publishers buy U.S. books and translate them into languages read around the world. You receive a royalty (usually from 5% to 10%) and they do the rest. Fortunately, you have a short cut to contacting foreign publishers. It's called *Right from the USA Review*. You can learn more about it by contacting:

Publishers Marketing Assn.
Jan Nathan, Director
2401 Pacific Coast Highway #102
Hermosa Beach, CA 90254
310-372-2732/Fax: 310-374-3342

NOTE: *For a complete discussion of the export and foreign rights market for self-publishers we recommend Dan Poynter's special report,* Exports/Foreign Rights, Selling U.S. Books Abroad *(available from Para Publishing for $19.95).*

Step 39. Brainstorm non-traditional markets— Quick, think of places you've seen books for sale outside of a bookstore. You have 60 seconds!

Now that you've got a short list, take a notebook with you the next time you've got a day full of errands. Really look around as you shop and then jot down every place you see books for sale.

Supermarkets, drugstores, pet shops, garden centers, health food and sporting good stores are typical examples. Think how much easier it would be to sell a book on cat care in a pet store than in a book store. Discover where your buyer hangs out. That's where your book belongs.

It's a fact: More books are sold in non-traditional settings than in all bookstores combined.

CASE STUDY: *Four Million Potential Buyers Every Year*

Don Parker, CEO of Conceivable Concepts (see Case Study in chapter two), creator of *Maternal Journal* and *Baby Journal,* markets these publications through maternity stores and gift shops, as well as bookstores. These markets were developed by attending trade shows, an idea Parker enthusiastically recommends. In addition to selling his books to retailers, his strategy was to make contact with publishers and distributors who specialized in the maternity field.

By good fortune, Meadowbrook Press, an affiliate of Simon & Schuster and one of the nation's largest publishers of prenatal care books (*What to Name the Baby, How to Be a Grandparent*, etc.), needed another strong new publication. By a joint-venture agreement, Parker inherited Meadowbrook's relationships, which included Simon & Schuster.

The agreement Parker negotiated gave him the entire distribution network of both Meadowbrook and Simon & Schuster, plus inclusion in both of their catalogs. Along with this came Meadowbrook's and Simon & Schuster's full staff of advertising and publicity people.

Although they had these relationships, Parker's associates still had to develop leads on their own before Meadowbrook/Simon & Schuster showed any real interest. It was Parker's partner Bennett who arranged appearances on Bill Cosby's "You Bet Your Life," "The Home Show," and placed an article in *People* magazine.

Endorsements and awards began coming from the American Diabetes Association, the March of

Dimes, the National Parenting Center and a number of other parenting organizations. Healthnet, a major national health maintenance organization, agreed to distribute *The Maternal Journal* nationwide. Parker's publishing company, Conceivable Concepts, is still a self-publisher, but now it has the fulfillment, distribution and publicity power of two giants behind it.

"We lucked out," Parker explained. "Our new partners in distribution had just missed several new-product deadlines and were facing a record low number of publications to offer their retailers that year. We came along with an exciting new idea which was readily available and just happened to fit perfectly into their marketing plans.

"Our original plan was to be selling at least 3,000 units per month by the end of the first year. Meadowbrook's support, the addition of the second book and the removal of the shrink-wrapping resulted in increased sales of the first book, making that figure reachable. We always knew the market was there, since our audience consists of over 4 million women giving birth every year in this country."

Parker confesses one of his mistakes was insisting on a minimum order of 24 units. Since it was an unknown product, a smaller minimum of six would have sold out sooner, creating the perception of a hot, easy-to-sell item instead of one that just sat there on the shelf for months.

Another regret was his hesitation to pre-sell. "We tied up all of our time in just producing it. We were unaware that pre-selling could really be done, and we lacked faith in our ability to meet a completion deadline. As a result, we started selling only after it was printed, thereby losing between six to nine months of valuable sales opportunities. That effort alone could have paid for the initial printing. Our cash reserves could have been better spent on the steps suggested in this book—news releases, pre-publication ads, announcements to key buyers, etc. This book would have been invaluable if we could have had it in the beginning of our book project."

Step 40. Research and develop a list of specialty book stores—
Approach specialty stores appropriate for your book. With your notebook full of research, compile a list of stores where your book could be sold. You'll find many are part of regional or national chains. Ask if you can "test market" your book in the local store, or find out if you need approval from the main office. Obviously it's quicker and easier to start locally. Explain your publicity plans. Be ready to create your own display and sign. A lucite picture frame works nicely for this purpose. Choose a 3" x 5" size. Use calligraphy or a desktop publishing format to write the name of the book, your name and a teaser phrase to create interest.

Example:

BOOK BLITZ
Getting Your Book in the News
by Barbara Gaughen and Ernest Weckbaugh

---

41. Mail brochure/flyer to targeted specialty book stores—
Remember your mail order techniques. You want your

envelope and letter to say, "Open me. Read me."

When you've already spoken to the person who will receive a letter from you, write a reminder on the envelope. You should write, "Enclosed is the information you requested" or "Thank you for your time on the phone today."

CASE STUDY: *The Brass Tooter*

Book publicist Irwin Zucker, president of Promotion in Motion, claims he may have more to do with a book becoming a best seller than the author. His Hollywood-based book publicity organization has tooted the brass for authors such as Jacqueline Susann and Helen Gurley Brown.

Now into his fifth decade in the publicity business, Zucker still maintains that no one can predict which books will become best sellers. He began his career as a publicist for Decca Records in New York City and spent the summer of 1952 in Europe as a foreign correspondent for *Billboard Magazine*. He put in three more years in New York with MGM Records as a public relations specialist before leaving for the West Coast to start his own business.

Year in and year out, Zucker's discovered that about ninety percent of the time (and this includes the best of candidates) book sales just don't happen without extensive promotion. He suggests that new authors start in local specialty book stores to gain experience in making public appearances.

"However, national television talk shows are by far the fastest way to make things happen," he says. "But an author must have developed the personality to be able to stay on the talk show trail and must feel a strong obligation to 'baby-sit' the book for as long as it takes."

Zucker also suggests obtaining some experience as a book publicist before tackling the chore of writing your own book. He recalls his most successful promotional campaign was for Joan Garrity who wrote *The Sensuous Woman,* which she then followed by writing and promoting *The Sensuous Man.* Her background included working as a publicist for Lyle Stuart, the firm which became her publisher. She spent years developing her skills working for other authors and getting paid for it by the very publisher who ultimately launched her first book. This went a long way toward making all of her achievements possible.

Another Zucker recommendation: "When you're preparing for an appearance on a talk show: Be sure to re-read (or at least scan) your current book, and any other books you've authored. Then you'll be able to give intelligent responses when your host, or those who phone in, begin asking questions that could embarrass you. The public expects total recall from you about every word you've ever written. You can't give an answer like, 'Gee, are you sure? I don't remember writing that.' That's about the fastest way there is to dry up any future talk show opportunities," Zucker warns.

CHAPTER ELEVEN

Enterprise Plus Premium Prize Equals Surprise!

—Chapter Eleven—
Choose the right company with a
product your book can help sell
and, in turn, their product
will help sell your book.

STEPS FORTY-TWO THROUGH FORTY-FIVE

Prior to printing . . .

42. Test other stores/markets with phone survey

43. Mail to catalog houses

44. Pursue premium offers

45. Pursue bookshelves

Step 42. Test other stores/markets with a phone survey—
Set aside a block of time on Tuesday through Thursday in the morning. By now you'll have a list of questions that help test the waters about interest in your book. Keep them next to the phone as you make your calls.

If a decision-maker is not available, don't think your call is in vain. You can get a lot of good information from clerks, secretaries, and other employees. Ask for their opinion and advice, but don't push it. If a person sounds reluctant to talk to you, empathize and say you will call back.

Unless you reach someone who seems genuinely interested in your information and in passing along the message, don't bother leaving your name and number. Instead, find out if there is a "best time" to call again.

The worst thing about leaving your name and number is that the decision-maker will call back when your mind is on a totally different subject. You won't remember why you made the original call which leaves the caller thinking you are disorganized (or worse).

Step 43. Mail to catalog houses—

With 7,000 catalog companies to chose from, the hard part is to narrow your choices. Fortunately, at least a dozen books exist that examine them for you. Check with the reference librarian for the titles that are available. Once you've determined the best markets for your book, send them a complimentary copy of your book with a tear sheet of an article about it. Add the latest information update in your cover letter and include your biography.

For your "second choices," send the cover letter and tear sheet only. If they want the book, have them fill out a (bounce back) Request for Merchandise Information Sheet and mail it back. Fill it out immediately and return it along with your book by first class mail or overnight delivery.

Step 44. Pursue premium offers—

Have you ever received a recipe book with a cooking appliance or a discount coupon with a box top? These are examples of "premium" or "incentive" sales. You get something that makes your purchase worth more. Books— especially nonfiction—are given with a variety of consumer goods and services. It's easy to see how a book on fitness could be matched with a "healthy" food product or a brand of athletic shoes . . . a wilderness guide book with a flashlight or batteries. If your book matches a company's needs, the sale of their product can carry it a long way.

To help find such a match, identify the categories of companies that are possible purchasers. Don't feel you can't compete with well-known authors and big publishing houses. Surprisingly, most don't even go after premium sales.

Premium sales can take months to negotiate from first interest to signed contract, so don't expect a quick decision.

Pay attention to commercials and print ads. Note what advertisers are saying and who they're saying it to. Then, read a few of the advertising trade journals to see what they're planning. If a credit card company is going after more female customers, they may consider a travel book for women. If a financial institution is looking for savings accounts, they may want to offer a book on budgeting.

With your "inside information," write a letter to the marketing director of the company. You'll find the name and address in the *Thomas Register of Manufacturers* at the Reference Desk of your library. While you're there, get the names of all competitors in the product category, too.

Send your book flyer, bio and an individual cover letter that explains how your book is an ideal companion to their marketing package. Mail these items with a bounce-back post card for quick response. Don't send the book, unless it is requested. All too often unsolicited books disappear from the mail room and never reach their intended party.

Three specialty magazines exist whose sole purpose is to match books with buyers. They are *Potentials in Marketing*, *Premium Incentive*, and *Inventive Marketing*. Check with the editor to find out their format for selecting books for review. If they judge your book to be worth inclusion, it will be seen by hundreds of potential buyers. They'll even keep track of companies that express interest in you.

Step 45. Pursue Book Shelves—

Get acquainted with as many bookstore owners as possible, especially those within driving distance of where you live. This is one of the best marketing moves you can make, especially with those who specialize in the type of book you're about to publish. Contact at least one of them on a daily basis and try to meet with them and their customers.

Personal Appearances

One of the best ways to accomplish this is through a personal appearance by you, the author, to autograph your book. But who arranges for that to happen?

"For book signings, the responsibility falls to a great extent on the author," says Barry Martin of BOOK 'Em Mysteries in South Pasadena, CA. "First, they need to be aggressive enough to contact us. We hear from local authors regularly. Publishers also call us about their mystery writers passing through on book tours from as far away as England, like Colin Dexter who writes the Inspector Morse mysteries currently airing on PBS's *Mystery Theater.* If authors don't call us, we don't call them, unless the author is someone we feel our customers would be particularly interested in, like Steve Allen, author of *The Murder Game* and *Murder in Vegas.* But, since we arrange and advertise from three to eight signings per month, there's plenty of opportunity for an author to do a book signing," says Martin.

Provide Personal Mailing Lists

"For publicity, we ask authors to provide us with the mailing addresses of people they know in our region, a list of up to fifty names. We add their list to our regular constituency to be used when our next monthly mailing goes out. This, of course, would be true of any bookstore in the country, assuming the author knows people within that store's local region. We always alert our own customers for any special events like these," he says.

One thing Martin strongly recommends is that authors pair-up and have a joint signing with two, even three writers of a similar specialty to share the audience. This is a greater drawing card for the writer (150 local friends instead of only 50) and is more efficient for the proprietor.

"The author has to realize how eager the bookstore owner is to sell his books," Martin says. "With book signings, depending on the importance of the author and the estimated volume of traffic, a small store may obligate itself for anywhere from 40 to 80 books per title."

How else can an author create a following and greatly increase in-store traffic?

Cooperative Advertising

"There is a vague term pubishers use called 'co-op dollars,' which can be very confusing for a bookseller," says Martin. "The ideal arrangement is where the publisher and the bookstore owner share the cost of setting up the public appearance of an author. Every publisher handles this disbursement in a different manner; each with its own rules and regulations. Some of the publisher's reps are quite good at getting money for a bookstore owner for the expense of advertising book signings. With others, you're on your own. It's their game and their rules.

"Small bookstore owners just don't have the time to plow through all those rules. They're too busy trying to operate their store and sell books. The author *could* be helpful in contacting their publisher for money, but it seldom happens," he says.

The owner's desire should be for the author to get more involved. Few bookstore proprietors would turn down your assistance if you could obtain co-op advertising cash for them.

The Book Fair Exposure

Schools often hold book fairs in cooperation with their local bookstores. Martin considers these to be very low-risk events for the bookstore owner, since the publishers offer a fully-returnable inventory for these events. This is yet another way for the new author to get exposure to a large audience of potential followers. These kinds of events have a long history of bookstores working with schools, providing teachers with educational material at discount and bringing the authors to the campus to meet the students. The American Booksellers Association can put an author in touch with regional booksellers associations and they, in turn, can provide lists of local specialty stores and book fair information.

"The point-of-view of the bookseller is critical to any author, especially a new one," Martin says. "We are the liaison between the author and the public when the author isn't available. It's very important, therefore, for every author to create as good a relationship with the management as they possible can. When a proprietor is considering which books to put in a customer's hands, the author needs to make sure his or her book is one of them.

CASE STUDY: *She Rescues Fallen Authors*

If you're looking forward to a best seller, and would like to know what happens when your book makes the best-seller list, listen to Doris Cross, the owner of TV Talent, a consulting firm in New York City. She regularly books appearances for two clients who have no lack of requests for their presence: Robert MacNeil (of the *MacNeil Lehrer NewsHour*) and Blanche Wiesen Cook, author of Eleanor Roosevelt, Volume 1, 1884-1933. Cook's publishers are Viking (hardcover) and Penguin (paperback). Cross worked for many years on MacNeil's show as a staff member and still handles all of his public appearances.

Says Cross about Blanche Cook's popularity, "There are no more than a few people a year who find themselves in such demand from the media. I mean, *besieged!* Blanche Cook told me she was almost at the point of taking both of her phones off the hook and disappearing somewhere due to the number of calls she was getting."

Through the recommendation of a mutual friend, she found Cross, who follows-up immediately on phone calls and written requests, even when the number is overwhelming. We should all be in such demand. But, even if your phone isn't ringing off the hook, you can still learn a lot from Cross' experiences.

"When a book first hits the bookstore shelves, you have that lovely 'Golden Period' with the publisher's publicist," Cross pointed out. "It's that brief moment in time when they're paying attention to you. But, even then, they won't help you think carefully through the strategy behind the publicity so that you can use it to your best advantage."

Here's where Doris Cross and her company come in to help coordinate activities for her clients. In a telephone conversation with Janet Kraybill, publicist for Penguin Books, Cross recalls saying, "What we both want to do is help Blanche and help her book sell. So, when it comes to scheduling interviews or public appearances, you let me know what you're doing and I'll let you know what I'm doing."

Cross knows all too well what usually happens next. It's her job to insure that the publicity runs smoothly and continuously for her clients. She has to be there when the publisher's publicist is assigned a new project.

Unless someone like Cross steps in, the author will feel abandoned and confused because they continue to get requests for appearances from the media directly, and indirectly through the publisher. If no one's in charge, they're not sure how to deal with the media or how to get the attention of their former friends in the publicity department at the publishing house.

"I keep a running list of contacts all over the country," Cross says, "so when the author goes out on tour I can make the most of the traveling they do. This is a 'quantity' business. Even a hot author is not making that much in terms of lecture fees. Consequently, I plan a very intense three or four week tour to make the most efficient use of my client's time during the trip. There's only one person—me— who has my client's schedule for the next year on my computer, so I need to update the publisher on agenda items as early as six months in advance." The publicity she gets for her clients has a direct affect on the publisher's distribution of their books.

Next to radio and television, colleges are one of Cross' favorite and most successful places for booking her clients. "The publicity staffs on campus usually have great contacts with the local press and can do a lot of the publicity work for you."

Cross has found that a concise, updated, one-page bio is enormously useful, since, for example, Cook's academic curriculum vitae is eight pages long. When Cook's book on Eleanor Roosevelt won the *Los Angeles Times Book Award* for "Best Biography for 1992," having her own short personal biography ready was essential to getting out the news release quickly. It also doubled as an introduction for her when she was asked to make speeches or appear on television.

CHAPTER TWELVE

Have Book, Will Travel

The Multi-purpose 3-1/2" x 5-1/2" Postcard— It can be an order form, a survey questionnaire, or a simple thank-you note.

Order Form

Book BLITZ, Getting Your Book in the News

	Number ordered	Total
Book BLITZ	___ x $12.95=	_____
California residents tax	. . . 1.07=	_____
Shipping and handling	. . . 3.00=	_____

Total amt. of check: _____

Ship to:

Name: _____

Address: _____

City: _____ State: ___ ZIP: _____
Telephone: ( ) _____

☐ Yes, I'd like information on seminars and seminar video.
Payment—Make check payable to Best-Seller Books.
Mail to: 226 E.Canon Perdido St., #B, Sta Barbara, CA 93101
or call in your toll-free order to **800-345-0096**

Best-Seller Books™
226 E. Canon Perdido, #B
Santa Barbara, CA 93101
(805) 965-8482

For details, see pages 167 and 168

—Chapter Twelve—
You've joined the likes of the
frequent flyers, the traveling salesmen,
a national touring company of players...
you've hit the road!

STEPS FORTY-SIX THROUGH FIFTY

After printing . . .

46. Your book is published

47. Send out advanced review copies to major media

48. Photograph book cover for press kits/post cards

49. Plan author tour, book signings, etc.

50. Target mailings to library/book trade publications

Step 46. Your book is published—

Have an autograph party. Invite your friends and colleagues. Send out news releases to the local press. Send invitations to the party to their social reporters.
Celebrate!!!

Tonight, old man, you did it! You did it! You did it!
You said that you would do it, and indeed you did...
From Act Two of My Fair Lady
by Alan Jay Lerner and Frederick Loewe

GETTING THE BUZZ ON!

Sinara Stull O'Donnell, whose case study *From Fear to Freedom* appears later in this chapter, spent twelve years with two major publishers. In that time, she observed authors who let the publisher do all the marketing and those who took matters into their own hands. Needless to say, in the latter case, the author-driven effort got the book's sales off to a great start.

O'Donnell describes the book party effort in this way: "In Hollywood, the 'In Crowd' is always talking about 'buzz.' Buzz is the word-of-mouth that precedes a movie. It can be negative and virtually destroy a movie's chances of doing well at the box office as it did with Madonna's 1992 movie *Body of Evidence* or, it can be positive as it was with Steven Spielberg's 1993 blockbuster hit *Jurassic Park*.

"As an author, you need to get the buzz going about your book," she suggests. "It is an overused phrase today, but you'll have to expand your 'network.' One way to do that is to throw a book party. Besides, you're going to feel like having a party after all the work you've done!"

O'Donnell breaks down the party into a series of steps:

1) Consider the costs. If you are self-published, you will probably have to foot the entire bill. If you are working with a major publisher, you may be able to arrange a co-op deal with them to cover expenses. Better still, they may cover all the expenses, including the invitations, food, beverages and the facility rental, although a private home is fine and has some definite advantages over a public hall.

Your publisher should at least provide books for you to sell. It is your choice as to whether you have a full dinner or just appetizers and dessert. Whatever you choose should be free to the guests. Pot-luck or a no-host bar is considered tacky.

2) Invite your world. Everyone you know should be

invited, from your mom to your boss to your best friends. If one person tells another and that person tells another, the buzz will quickly spread. Even if your book is on a subject your best friends aren't interested in, they will still want to own your book. "My best friend wrote this!" they'll say. Likewise, your family and associates will be proud to be part of the celebration.

3) Invite the local press. Neighborhood newspapers will often send their social-scene reporters to this kind of an event, especially when they hear about the free food. Now you've added the print media to you buzz, and for free! Besides, your mom and friends will be thrilled to be in the paper!

4) Invitations should be formal, but warm and welcoming. They can be simple and hand-written if your list is small. For a larger crowd, however, you can either go with a simple, cleverly-written invitation on

---

You are cordially invited to
a party celebrating the publication of

Book Blitz—

Getting Your Book in the News
by Barbara Gaughen
and Ernest Weckbaugh

Date: _____

Place: _____

RSVP

---

colored paper all the way to a more elegant-appearing printed card (see above). The latter are available at fairly moderate prices from most printers or copy centers.

5) Have others blow your horn. It is advisable to present a short program about midway through the festivities. This could feature three or four speakers who have followed your progress over the months or years and might discuss their participation in the event. The speakers could be your co-authors, reviewers, editors, publicists, your agent, a good friend or relative and, of course, YOU!

6) Take your bows. You deserve it! The writing is finally done and you would like to hear applause, not to mention the ring of cash registers! At this point, you need to welcome the audience and thank them for coming. Thank those who have helped you along the way. Don't forget to thank those nearest and dearest to you who have had to put up with long hours and short tempers. You may also wish to thank certain professionals who assisted in the process.

7) Sell books! Although you may wish to give selected people autographed copies, your purpose in writing books should be to *sell* books, not give them away. Have a table set up with books for sale. You should not personally handle the money, but be sure to be on hand to autograph copies.

8) Have fun! This is your chance to celebrate the end of the grueling writing process and the beginning of the best-seller phase of your book.

If you have a large out-of-town mailing list of people you want to inform about the completion of your book (your Christmas card list, for example), you may wish to send out a flyer or postcard announcing the book's publication. This should include the title, your name, the date it will be available, the publisher's name or how to order if self-published, the cost and the ISBN number for ease in ordering through a bookstore. ISBN stands for International Standard Book Number, a numerical designation unique to every book, which makes it easier for bookstores to identify it for ordering purposes.

Step 47. Send advance review copies to major media— These are the major TV shows, national magazines, and high circulation newspapers that reach thousands, even millions of people at once.

Include an updated news release that incorporates any news that will make you or your book more appealing. Have you received an award? Will the book shed light on an issue or part of the world that's been in the news? Lead with your hottest topic. Write it on the outside of a colored envelope. This should result, with a little follow-up, in some invitations to be interviewed on "What's His Name's" talk show (radio or TV) or a call from the local newspapers.

Step 48. Photograph cover for press kits, postcards— A photograph of the book itself helps people identify what it looks like so they can find it in a bookstore. Once you have

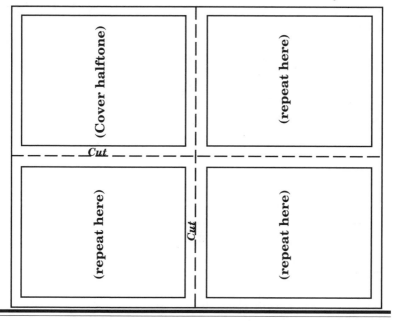

the cover photo, if you first turn it into a *halftone* print, to make it possible to reproduce, you can make your own postcards. To create the postcards, start with an 8-1/2" x 11" sheet of paper. Divide it into quarters with a light blue non-reproducing pencil (see illustration on last page). Each section is now the "master" for a postcard. Place your cover halftones on one side and return address on the other in each one of the four rectangles. Experiment with your word processor or ask the people at your favorite copy shop for help. Finally, have both sides reproduced (see below for the back side) on pastel-colored cover stock and cut into fourths. A reduced-size version of the cover halftone can also be used on stationery, envelopes, business cards, and stickers. (For further tips on postcards see Case Study: *Sharing Some Ideas* later in this chapter.)

(Your return address)	*(Place stamp here)*
(Your message, or a thank you note)	*(Addressee)*

You'll find these 4-1/4" x 5-1/2" postcards are ideal for quick thank-you notes, reminders and follow-ups. If you vary from this size, be sure you check postal regulations for allowable card sizes. Keep them stacked, stamped and close by. You can also duplicate the book's cover photo like you did your own photograph to send to the media. It can serve as a logo. You can glue it to the front of the folder, creating a handsome press kit, or ask your publisher if they have extra book covers for the same purpose. Carolyn See, book reviewer for the *Los Angeles Times* and author of *Golden Days* and *The Rest Is Done With Mirrors* (among others) from Fawcett Crest, tells writers to "Write one charming note each day" to build up their circle of people who will help make their work successful.

Step 49. Plan author tour, book signings, etc.— Get out your calendar, organizer or computer schedule now, because this is where details count. Start with a sure thing, even if it's a visit to Aunt Mary. Research every place you'll visit in the next 12 months. Find out what bookstores, speaking locations, or other promotion possibilities might be available to you. Enlist friends, relatives and colleagues to help. Maybe you can speak at Cousin Edna's book circle or Uncle Henry's lodge. If you know someone who is outgoing, ask if they'll call local bookstores and community groups on your behalf. From your own phone experience, you can prepare a script for them. It's always better if someone other than yourself can speak about you in glowing terms. But don't seem too available. Make it appear that you're in demand.

TIP: When the person asking you to speak wants to set up a date and time, suggest two or three possibilities.

Go back to the library's reference desk. Thumb through the *Yellow Pages* and *Encyclopedia of Associations* for the area you're going to visit for speaking possibilities. Then have your "committee" call and make contact with the decision-makers of the various associations in each area about booking you to speak.

CASE STUDY: *Throwing Up in Madison*

Author Marlys Milhiser writes that when she returned from two back-to-back tours, she was "brimming with cogent thoughts and radical ideas about self-promotion."

Her comments:

"They are sending the wrong people on book tours! The ones who actually need to get out into the real world are agents and those from the marketing, sales, publicity and editing departments of the publisher. Leaving New York for a few days to visit a book convention or two doesn't give anyone a true picture of what's going on out there. Even speaking at writers' conventions, or visiting the ABA Conventions, or talking to salesmen who've talked to area reps who've talked to bookstore staff members doesn't cut it either.

"One of the newest wrinkles in the constant battle to prove oneself promotable to an indifferent publisher is to hire a New York publicist or, second best, one in your own area who'll be more affordable, or one in the area in which your book is set. It's worth noting that nobody's making authors do this. But the fact is, writing skills are not all that rare and you need to stand out in a very crowded field, hoping that Lady Luck will take notice."

Is it all worth it? Or would authors make better use of their time and energy by staying home writing and just depending on chance to sell their books. Ms. Milhiser can honestly say she's glad she took these tours, if only for the experiences.

"I walked into a brand new bookstore in Chicago unannounced and found my book there," she recalls. "I passed a B. Dalton in a Las Vegas mall and saw copies I'd previously signed displayed face out at the front of the store. I had the thrill of meeting fans, both old and potential, who would probably never make it to a convention. I did a talk and reading in Albuquerque on a Saturday night and realized that people who had simply wandered in to browse had stopped to listen. Many of them stayed to ask questions, some even bought books."

Yes, but would she do it again?

"That's a little harder to answer," she says. "On the Midwest tour, we hit one bookstore that had had almost 30 writers come through during the previous year. We had a good crowd for our panel discussion, but the sales were lower than expected. Bookstore owners everywhere had us sign all their copies and assured us that they would all sell before Christmas. All of them were kind and wonderful people, but we also realized they had to be good business people to survive.

"But the dilemma remains. A writer cannot really afford to promote, yet cannot afford not to. Promotion certainly will not improve writing skills, but it does allow a writer to continue to publish."

Another thought she offered is to blanket the region in which you live. Before you take on a national book tour, send your book with your brochures or press kits and follow-up with phone calls to every bookstore, novelty shop, newspaper, radio, TV and cable show in your own area and in three or four adjacent states. After getting that experience behind you, you should be ready for the "big time."

Even the bad parts of a tour, however, can be most memorable.

"There was a violent flu bug that attacked our little group in the Midwest. It was the low point in our national tour," Milhiser vividly remembers. "After it was over, we labeled the episode *Throwing Up In Madison*. But, in spite of it all, we really had a blast!"

Step 50. Target mailing to library/book trade publications—

Libraries are a great market that can boost your name recognition and credibility.

If your book has an outside publisher this step will be done for you. If you're self-publishing, send galleys to *Booklist, Library Journal* and *American Libraries* (see Gray Pages). A good review in any of these journals will insure pre-publication sales.

TIP: The topic of your next book could come from research into subjects that are a scarcity among books in print.

CASE STUDY: *Sharing Some Ideas*

What happens if your book cover doesn't photograph well when you reduce its size? Dottie Walters and Lillie Walters, co-authors of *Speak and Grow Rich* (published by Prentice Hall/Simon Schuster), solved this problem by pasting their pictures on the front of the actual book, covering the smaller type and leaving just their names and the title showing. "Then we had a sharp-contrast print taken by a professional photographer and had several thousand glossy black-and-white prints made by a quantity photolab," Dottie

Walters explained.

"Next, we obtained a copy of *Publications in Print* from R.R. Bowker (121 Chanlon Road, New Providence, NJ 07974, [908] 464-6800) and called every editor of any listed publication with a tie-in to the subject of our book—professional public speaking. We asked if they might consider giving us a book review or an article. Over half of them said yes! So we sent the material to them, including one of our modified glossy pictures of the cover of the book. Most of them used the picture, probably because it was the right size—one column wide. We had made it easy for them to use it. Each one of the reviews told how the book could be purchased and ran our address at the end of the article.

"Next we used the cover photos, printed in a 5" x 7" size, on the front of shiny red folders, which created an inexpensive but great looking press kit," she explained. "We bought the folders from wholesale stationery suppliers by the box as we needed them. We then advertised in the Bradley Communications magazine, *Radio-TV Interview Report: The Magazine Producers Read to Find Guests* (Box 1206, Lansdowne, PA 19050) which is very inexpensive and is mailed to all radio, television and print media in the United States. We offered phone interviews on a subject we called "Money in your mouth and gold on the tip of your tongue!" by the authors of the book *Speak and Grow Rich*.

"As each issue of the magazine is mailed out, we receive a flood of phone calls inviting us to appear on talk shows. We send each show producer a copy of our press kit and a nice thank you note to both the show's producer and to its host.

We mail a copy of this thank you letter to our book editor and to the publicity department of Prentice Hall. We want to let our publisher know of our efforts. They've always been very cooperative with us in every way, since we make sure they know how hard we work at promoting 'our book.' We also sent them copies of all of the articles we've written and the reviews and comments about the book from every publication world wide," she said.

"One of the radio stations who interviewed us asked if we would do an interview for their network show. This turned out to be so successful they asked me if I would do a program on a regular basis for their broadcasting syndicate, the Business Radio Network. My show is now heard on over 100 major stations across the country on a daily basis.

"Another thing that has proven to be very successful for us has been the publication of *Sharing Ideas Newsmagazine,* on the subject of paid speaking, which now has an international readership. We originally sold it on a one-year basis only. But then we decided to offer a two-year subscription and include an autographed copy of the book *Speak and Grow Rich.* Since we eliminate the expense of re-soliciting the second-year subscription and we buy the books wholesale, the book-premium idea both saves us a lot of money in renewal costs and provides our subscribers with a valuable gift. We have many new subscribers every week, which means a stream of books go out constantly," she said.

"Still another way we sell them is by offering the books at the back of the room after every speaking engagement. Members of the audience buy them as they leave. We also sell them in advance when we're booked by a client, so that every person who comes to the event receives an already autographed copy," Walters said. "In this case, we offer them at a quantity discount. *Speak and Grow Rich* and Lilly Walters' new book *Successful Speakers: How to Motivate, Captivate and Persuade (Presentation Secrets of the World's 60 Top Speakers)* published by McGraw Hill (selected by both Fortune Business Book Club and The Book of the Month Club for their catalogs) are also featured in a free catalog we produce which includes other books, tapes and videos on the same subject."

What if you're **not** a Dottie Walters, who enjoys public speaking? How do you overcome stage fright? If you realize that getting up in front of an audience is inevitable, what choices do you have? Performance anxiety is the number one fear known to man, and woman. Your only choice is to learn how to deal with it.

CASE STUDY: *From Fear to Freedom*

Sinara Stull O'Donnell has a habit of saying to herself just before she goes on the stage, "I'm not nervous, I'm just excited, thank you."

When she got a part in her first play as an adult, 13 years after graduating from Whittier College with a B.A. in Speech and Drama (she received an M.A. in Communication from the University of Arizona), she was petrified with fear. "I had auditioned for a small character role and I got the lead! In fact, I had more lines to memorize than anyone else in the play!

"As I stood backstage with the actor who played my husband, my legs were shaking," she says. "I whispered to him, 'I'm so nervous.' He whispered back, 'No you're not, you're just excited.' Those words changed my life."

Since then she has developed three careers: one as a marketing representative for both Prentice-Hall and McGraw-Hill, where she performed sales and field-editing functions; another as a television actress on *Cheers* and *General Hospital*, on stage in plays as a serious actress and in comedy clubs as a stand-up comic; and yet another career as a corporate trainer and career-development counselor. She's performed before audiences ranging from 20 to 2000 and is currently a member of both the Screen Actor's Guild and AFTRA. Currently, she is a free-lance writer with articles that have appeared in such diverse publications as the *Wall Street Journal National Business Employment Weekly, Lady's Circle, 'Teen, Sacramento Magazine,* etc.

"In order for a book to sell," O'Donnell says, "the author must take center stage. In publishing, the post-production period *is* 'showtime.' You, the author, like an actor, have to be ready to perform. There are audiences waiting for you, and you had better be excited about the prospect of appearing in front of these large groups of people.

"It is a fact that many of today's most competent performers have been extremely shy prior to developing their performance skills, and some of them still fight this kind of anxiety on a daily basis. Perhaps you've heard yourself saying things like, 'If I just hold my breath, time will stand still and I won't have to go up there.' If not, you are in a rare minority. Most of the rest of us have had 'performance anxiety' to some degree at least one time in our life. 'Stage fright' is as common as an occasional bout of the blues, and who hasn't felt down from time to time?" she wonders.

"But you as a writer have several advantages. No matter how inexperienced or how polished a public speaker you are, it is always easier to talk about your favorite subject. It's safe to assume that a newborn book, like a newborn child or grandchild, would be any author's favorite thing to talk about. One writer recently expressed his current condition as 'being great with book,' as near as any man can experience the feeling of being pregnant.

"No one knows the material and the background of your book better than you do, O'Donnell maintains. "But it's important to learn the skills necessary to present that knowledge effectively.

"Too often I've seen audiences squirm in the presence of an author who won't look up and whose hands and voice are shaking," she says. "They read their material as if they're seeing it for the first time in a voice that has all the forcefulness of an adolescent asking for his first date. A person like this should be looking for help."

Much of an author's timidity is due to the nature of the writing task being so solitary. Unfortunately, once the manuscript is completed, it must be sold to an agent, to a publisher and, ultimately, to an audience of their salespeople or buyers and the general public.

What you need to do is take that same enthusiasm which prompted you to complete the manuscript and use it to drive you through the other steps in the final phase of the project, the part that comes after the writing is over. Simply stated, now you need to sell your book.

Here are 10 steps that O'Donnell suggests to help you overcome any stage fright you may be suffering in anticipation of facing an audience of one, or one thousand:

1. Tell yourself, "I am so excited!" rather than "I am so frightened." Excitement is the positive form of the same feeling we experience when we're afraid. It anticipates a challenge and has energy, if the adrenaline in your body can be kept under control.

Fear comes from the unknown aspect of performing and causes withdrawal, an attitude which can be seen in your actions. Your inexperience and lack of practice account for it. It is often so overwhelming that the flight reaction takes over and, rather than standing up and fighting it, you run.

2. Rehearse. Practice speaking in every situation you can find over a number of months, even a year or two. If your church needs a Sunday school teacher-volunteer, or if the local chapter of the Diabetes Association needs volunteers to go around and speak before clubs and organizations to raise money, do it! Join a local chapter of a mutual-help speech organization like Toastmasters, International. The improvement among those who have the courage to stay past the first few talks is a remarkable thing to see. The opportunities to perform before an understanding and sympathetic audience, the chance to learn to "think on your feet," the example of members who've overcome their fears, and the evaluations you get to help you eliminate flaws in your presentation are all invaluable.

While you're doing this, keep in mind your ultimate goal—selling your book. After you practice speaking, gradually learn to relax, become used to the sound of your own voice, and realize how much fun it is to entertain an audience, you'll be ready.

3. Be thoroughly prepared. It may be cliché, but "Do

your homework!" is probably the best advice your
mother ever gave you. Learn your material thoroughly
and practice the presentation you're about to give to
your editor the same way you would a speech. Say it
aloud to the mirror, your family, your dog, and into your
tape recorder, then carefully listen to yourself. In the
case of your editor, you have to be able to convince an
audience of one person the same way as you would an
audience of 100. The title of *this* speech should be, "Who
will buy my book, where will it sell and why."

4. Find out about the person or the group you'll be
addressing. Before you arrive to sell your idea to a
publisher or, a year or two later, to sell the finished
book to an eager convention where you are the keynote
speaker, learn as much as you can about your publisher
or about your convention audience. This kind of research is among the most important you'll ever do as a
writer. The better you know them, and the sooner you
realize they are no different than anyone else, the more
comfortable and effective you'll be.

5. Practice deep breathing before entering an interview room or ascending a dais. It has a calming effect
and helps to remind you to stand or sit erect, with an
attitude of being in command of the situation.

6. Get plenty of sleep the night before and make sure
you have a good breakfast. "Once, before an important
presentation, I overslept," O'Donnell recalls. "In my
hurry I missed breakfast. After I had begun my presentation, I had to bend over to pick up a pencil. I almost
passed out. I had to give my audience a ten-minute
break so I could eat a candy bar. Now I always grab
something to eat no matter how late I've slept."

7. It's okay to talk about your fear—but **not** to the
audience! When a speaker apologizes, saying "Please
excuse me, I'm very nervous," the whole audience is
suddenly on pins and needles worrying about what to

expect next. Will he or she "blow it?" How embarrassing is this going to be? I wish I hadn't come tonight, etc. That's a lot of negative energy to try to overcome.

If you feel yourself stumbling, just pause and remain calm. Take a moment to find your place, then go on. What may seem like an eternity to you will hardly be noticed by the audience if you don't point it out.

8. Practice creative visualization. Try to "see" yourself in front of your audience. "See" yourself standing, walking to the podium, calmly putting down your material, looking at the audience and beginning your speech. "See" the faces of friendly members of your audience smiling up at you and supporting every word you say. O'Donnell remembers an actress friend who would play a tape of applause every day on the way to the theatre to "psyche" herself up.

9. Remember, *you* are an authority! You are there to sell a book that you, the expert, have written. You are the "inventor" of this product. Nobody on the face of the earth knows more about it than you do.

10. Don't lose your sense of humor. No matter what goes wrong, if nothing else, this experience will make a great story someday.

CHAPTER THIRTEEN

Shout It
in
The Library!

Review:

Building a Best Seller . . . by Yourself!

Ask authors Barbara Gaughen and Ernest Weckbaugh how best sellers are made and they're liable to tell you to "do it yourself."

That's the message contained in their book, *Book Blitz, Getting Your Book In The News* ($12.95 from Best-Seller Books, ISBN 1-881474-02-X, telephone 805/965-8482). The guts of this handy 268-page tome are the authors' description of their very specific, hands-on book marketing approach, which they call "60 Steps to a Best Seller." Readers learn how to prepare press kits, develop and mail self-promoting brochures, contact libraries and foreign publishers, do telephone surveys, offer premiums, deal with the media, and many more ways to push their books to the top of the list.

The authors are no lightweights when it comes to promotion and show biz. Gaughen, an international PR practitioner, is a four-time winner of Business Digest's "Best of Business Award." She is also the author of *Getting the World to Beat a Path to Your Door*. Weckbaugh, an accomplished author and ghostwriter, began his working career at the ripe old age of 5, when he signed on as a child actor with Warner Bros. (His credits include several appearances in the later episodes of the Our Gang Comedies.)

Writing for Money, February 28, 1994

—Chapter Thirteen—
If you've ever enjoyed spending
time in a library, now is
when it begins to pay off.

STEPS FIFTY-ONE THROUGH FIFTY-SIX

After printing . . .

51. Research special editions of library review magazines

52. Send books to library review magazines

53. Donate your book to local libraries and publicize

54. Send review copy to general media

55. Sell book directly to appropriate local retailers

56. Follow-up with media

Step 51. Research special editions of library review magazines—

There is an entire category of magazines that publish book reviews for libraries. Ask the Reference Librarian to find their current listings. Most of these magazines print "special editions" which spotlight specific topics. Once you've found out what these upcoming topics are going to be, mail information on your book where it best suits or matches their focus.

A good review here could sell thousands of copies. Librarians and book dealers alike look to this category of magazines the same way movie-goers trust Siskel and Ebert.

Step 52. Send books to library review magazines— Most library review magazines will work from either the galleys or the finished book. Check listings to find out the specifics. Don't wait to send the finished product unless they specifically request it. Twelve to fifteen weeks is not an unusual lead time for a review. Remember, editors need to allow time for writing as well as printing just like you do.

Send a cover letter that explains how your book benefits its target audience and why it is unique in the marketplace. Show that you are informed about each publication you approach by demonstrating how your book will fit in the special edition schedule.

Step 53. Donate your book to a local library and publicize—
In this era of cutbacks, libraries are eager for donations, especially a gift from a local author. To make the most of your donation, call ahead and find out the procedure first. Most libraries have "support groups," sometimes called "Friends of the Library." These are people who donate funds and meet to discuss book topics. Ask if you can make a presentation about your book to them. If so, find out if the public can attend. Suggest to them that the topic of your book would attract an audience and draw attention to their library membership drive.

Create a fanfare. Send out a news release about the event. Let the whole town and surrounding area know about it. Then culminate your speech with a presentation of the book with an added bonus. Spend a few dollars for a book display stand. Add a small sign that states your name, the name of the book and the words, "Read it here or ask for it at your favorite bookstore."

CASE STUDY: *The Magic Storybag*

Lael Littke, the author of approximately 30 books for young people, found that she could get a lot of exposure for her books by speaking at schools during district authors festivals or young authors conferences. The trick is to get your name on the list of authors invited to be presenters (see invitation at the end of this Case Study).

"You could start by volunteering to talk about your book to children at a local school," Littke says. "Or if you know someone who is taking part in district authors festivals, you could get the name of the person who runs the event and ask to have your name added to the list of invited authors."

Principals and teachers are usually very receptive to anyone who can encourage reading skills, promote use of the libraries, both school and public, and develop interest in creative writing. You might speak to people involved in the literacy program in your own district about sponsoring an authors festival. Many authors would be invited to come speak so that all the children in the district could hear one and learn that books are written by real people.

This, of course, will cost money, so the PTA will need to be brought into the picture. Most districts that sponsor authors festivals offer each author $100 for the day's work, and most PTA organizations agree that it's money well spent.

Storytellers are always popular, especially those who are skilled at involving children in the creative process of writing the story. Littke's friend, author Caroline Arnold, writes non-fiction animal stories and often visits schools and libraries to speak to both children and adults. She uses her books, such as *Cheetah* and *Peregrine Falcon,* to teach not only about these beautiful creatures, but also how to use the library to research facts and create stories about them. She conducts a hands-on workshop which shows students how a book is created from idea to printed page.

Watching an artist at work is as fascinating to children as it is to adults. Book illustrator Virginia Fleming often works in both school and public libraries, showing youngsters and their parents her techniques for illustrating books. She even has them drawing right along with her. She, like the author storytellers, makes the stacks of books come alive for young imaginations.

Littke brings a "magic storybag" with her whenever she visits children in a classroom or school library. Filled with such intriguing items as a crystal ball (a glass flotation sphere used in commercial fishing), an oversized toothbrush (found in a dental visual-aid kit), and an Aladdin's lamp (purchased in a gift store), she opens the bag's drawstring and pulls them out, one-by-one, to start the youngster's imaginations soaring.

With each item she asks them:
- Who might use this? *(development of a character);*
- What difficulty does the person have who has this thing? *(problem);*
- What obstacle does he or she face in making use of it? *(conflict);*
- How does he or she get around the difficulty or obstacle? *(solution);*
- What's learned from the experience? *(object lesson).*

"With this little game, I teach them the basic formula for writing fiction. Through it all, their enthusiasm and personal involvement creates a high level of fun," Littke testifies.

The crystal ball, for example, might suggest a gypsy fortune teller. Littke immediately asks the children what the fortune teller's name is. One idea leads to another and a story is born as she teaches them the basic techniques of a professional writer.

Opportunities like this are often available, serving both to promote your book and to pay you well for the time spent. Contact the school district's main office, public libraries or bookstores. Find the people who are the prime movers in each of these organizations and work closely with them. They will be able to arrange for a published author like yourself to visit children in the classroom during the school day. Bookstore owners and school and public librarians should give you enthusiastic support.

Be sure the plan for publicizing your appearance is under your control. Supporting a good cause is sufficient to get the attention of newspaper editors, as long as you approach them courteously and professionally. It may even be worth several comments on local television. In larger metropolitan areas, the television and newspaper people aren't too interested unless there is some kind of powerful "hook." See if the newspaper has a regional edition. Prior to your presentation, signs need to be hung in the district's schools, the local bookstores and the public libraries. A well-organized committee from the PTA or literacy group can do all of this if you help them put together a detailed plan. The signs should include when and where you'll be available to autograph your books.

Teachers are usually thrilled to introduce you, a "celebrity," to their classes, especially if you help the teacher by preparing a follow-up lesson plan to sustain the students' interest in books and writing for weeks to follow.

A school or PTA has been known to pay as much as $100 to $300 per day for two to four hours of your time. An entire day, spent with a half-dozen classes for about 45 minutes each, has been known to bring in as much as $500 in some districts with an interesting author—one who has been successful in the classroom. This can be a wonderful warm-up practice for more lucrative or challenging speaking engagements or interviews. It can also be a real confidence-building experience. The emphasis on increasing our national literacy rate, increasing the use of our public libraries and enhancing our young people's ability to read makes this a particularly important promotional opportunity.

There are several payoffs here for the publicity-minded writer. The school library will usually buy several of your books for their inventory. The children may bring money from home to buy your books, if they're told about it in advance. Be sure to check the legal issues and school policies in advance. An autograph signing after school can be arranged where the parents can meet you, receive a mail order form or buy your books on the spot. Of course, they *pay* you to appear at the school. Then when it comes to book signing appearances at the local bookstores, if you've become better known as a result of the attendant publicity in the newspapers or from the direct-mail flyers from the children's literacy organization, the local bookstore management is far more eager to be involved because he can expect a larger crowd.

At a later date, you may also want to accompany the class, on a field trip to one of the supporting bookstores. This is a perfect opportunity to introduce prospective buyers (teacher, parents and students) to the local bookstore owner, manager and staff.

See if a local TV or radio station will cover it, or a newspaper will report this effort to promote literacy.

LONG BEACH Authors Festival

Ms. Lael J. Littke
1345 Daveric Drive
Pasadena, CA 91107

Dear Ms. Littke:

As you no doubt recall, the Long Beach Authors Festival was named the winner of the prestigious Golden Bell Award presented annually by the California School Boards Association! As one of our authors whose participation led to our winning this award, you are invited to honor us with your presence again this year on WEDNESDAY, MARCH 30, 1994 for our seventeenth annual AUTHORS FESTIVAL, a cooperative venture co-sponsored by the Long Beach Unified School District, the Long Beach Public Library, the Zonta Club and other local civic organizations.

In recognition of the value of your contributions, our Committee has voted to continue the honorarium of $100.00 for participating in this award-winning event which is supported solely by contributions from our community groups.

This year's Festival will again provide a rewarding and stimulating opportunity: you will spend much of the day as an "author-in-residence" in a school within our district, talking with youngsters in large and/or small groups about the art of writing and the joys of reading. This experience will be exciting for the students and, we hope, delightful for you as well. Your books will be featured at the school you visit and youngsters will be informed of your works prior to the Festival.

Schools will make individual arrangements to provide opportunities for one-to-one contact between authors and students as well as for sales of your books during a Reception held on campus after school. Your school's Festival Representative will contact you in February regarding this and the other day's activities.

We sincerely hope that you will consent to join us. However, whether or not you are able to be with us, we would appreciate your completing the enclosed information sheet and returning it to us no later than NOVEMBER 1,1993. This information will assist teachers and librarians in preparing students for your visit. If you are able to join us, you will receive other communications with more details. We look forward to hearing from you and hope that you will join us for our award-winning event.

Sincerely,

Nancy Messineo, Co-chairman
Youth Services Officer
Long Beach Public Library

Joan Hansen
Festival Chairman

Joan Hansen

Marilyn Larson, Co-chairman
District Lib. Media Spec.
L.B.U.S.D.

Enclosures

Sponsored by

Long Beach Unified School District • Long Beach Public Library • Los Angeles County Library

Long Beach School District PTA's • Zonta Club of Long Beach

Step 54. Send review copy to general media—
There have been incidents where review copies have been stolen in the mail room and never reached the intended reader. However, a well-researched reviewer list should eliminate most possibilities of "booknapping" (see Gray Pages section).

Literary Market Place is a good source of book reviewers and critics. Many of them syndicate their column to many of the smaller markets, helping you cover a lot of the country with a single mailing.

Include your brochure, a sample news release, and other reviews if you have them, You can also include a post card that states options the reviewer might take.

PLEASE ACKNOWLEDGE

We have received the complimentary review book or galleys you sent of

Book title: _____

☐ We expect to review this book on (date): _____
☐ Please send a photograph of the book
☐ Please send a photograph of the author
☐ We did not find this book suitable for our review.

Name of reviewer: _____
Full job title: _____
Name of publication or broadcast station: _____
Mailing address: _____
_____ Zip: _____
Comments (optional): _____

(Courtesy of Para Publishing)

Step 55. Sell book directly to appropriate local retailers—
Although wholesalers can bring you big returns with little effort, there's a real high from making a direct sale on the local level. Even though you have a wholesaler/distributor, this doesn't stop you from selling directly to other stores, etc., that are not sold to by them. These

retailers are either out of their territory or in a retail category they don't list as customers. For example, if your book is on pets, your local petstore is probably not on most book wholesaler/distributors mailing list.

In addition, contact with the people who actually buy and sell your book will provide insight into your customers and how to get them to say "yes."

These local booksellers benefit too, because you can provide books without a shipping charge and will be glad to autograph each and every copy, greatly enhancing their value when sold.

Call ahead for an appointment with the store manager or buyer. Let that person know that, unlike sales reps who usually carry only book covers, you travel with the *Real McCoy*. When you meet, be sure to talk about your publicity plans. Show your press clippings or quotes to show how well you have been keeping your end of the sales bargain.

Step 56. Follow-up with media—

When the people in Barbara Gaughen's Public Relations Workshops are told to make follow-up calls to the media, you can feel a palpable gasp. Yet this one step can result in the most rewards for the persistent caller.

A sincere call to the press with an interesting, newsworthy message is *not* an intrusion. Gwen Carden, free-lance writer, says she even enjoys some of the calls.

These are not calls where you plead for space or chastise an editor for not publishing your release. We're talking about a give-and-take conversation where you find out what the reporter's looking for and find a way to meet the need...where you explain how part of your book ties in with a *hot* current event...and where you use your writer's creativity to capture the reporter's imagination.

If your information doesn't match his or her needs

right now, accept the fact graciously, ask if *another* reporter might be interested, thank them, and get off the phone.

CHAPTER FOURTEEN

Party, Party!

—Chapter Fourteen—
Now is the time for
all good friends to come
to your aid at your party...
and buy an autographed book!

STEPS FIFTY-SEVEN THROUGH SIXTY

After printing . . .

57. *Arrange local media promotion/autograph parties*

58. *Research/develop co-op promotion with bookstore*

59. *Offer book to major publishers for reprint*

60. *Review this book monthly, read the books listed in*
**   *the Gray Pages section, and start a daily program***
**   *of continuing self-education***

Step 57. Arrange media promotion/autograph parties—

Unless you live in Manhattan, your local press is probably
comprised of rookie reporters getting their first break and
an "old-timer" or two who love the town and will never
leave. None of them earn a lot and few get many perks. If
you want to get their attention, have an event on Tuesday
or Wednesday. (Make sure you don't choose the day when
the City Council or the Board of Supervisors meet.) Serve

snacks and beverages. Give a short presentation. Hand out a one-page release that re-caps your presentation. If a reporter or photographer expresses interest, autograph a book and give it to him or her. If they don't seem that interested, hand them a photo of the cover.

Autograph parties might get press coverage in the local newspaper's social column. Parties can also gain publicity if a portion of the book sale proceeds go to a local charity. A charitable contribution can sometimes gain the attention of, or a connection with, the celebrity who has loaned their name value to the cause. If that celebrity is able to accept an invitation to the festivities, that same name value can attach to your book when the local press writes it up.

Step 58. Research and develop co-op promotion with bookstores—

Firm up your book signing dates. Find out what sort of advertising each book store is prepared to do to promote you. Don't assume anything. Check with your publisher to see if co-op funds are available and learn how to complete the paperwork to get them. Volunteer to write a news releases for the events. Tell them you'll be glad to mention that your book is available for sale at their store in interviews and releases.

Find out if they have a direct mail flyer or a promotional booklet in which your book can appear. Volunteer to write the review and supply a photo of the cover, if necessary.

On the day of your book signing, see if you can autograph every single volume of your book in the store, not just the ones that are sold that day. This gives the books extra value. You may even suggest that they be displayed in a special way in the store. More importantly, it means that none of those books can be returned for a refund.

Step 59. Offer book to major publishers for reprint—

Once is not enough when it comes to publishing. Major publishing houses purchase self-published books that fit their product line. Paperback publishers pick up books that someone else has printed in hardcover.

Major publishers have years of experience in "deal making." Unless you have the expertise to do so yourself, be sure you either have an attorney or someone knowledgable in business speak for you. In this situation, ignorance is not bliss.

If you are a first-time author, don't expect too many concessions. One thing you can almost always get is royalties on a quarterly basis rather than annually.

TIP: Let the publisher know you have updated material to add that will keep your book current.

PUBLISHING AS AN INVESTMENT

Most writers, when they start a project, probably don't think of themselves as investors. But, before any wise author begins, a thorough assessment of the "target market" should be made (Who would want to buy a book like this?). This is no different than any smart real estate investor who sizes up a piece of income property before buying.

The question you should ask is, "Is there a possibility, by studying the market (a specific segment of the book-buying public) and making improvements (researching and finishing the book with that target audience in mind) that I can turn this property (book) into something profitable?"

The reality is that authors are directly responsible for the return on their investment, far more than the average investor. Whether you lose your investment or it makes a profit depends on your in-depth understanding of your potential reader, the value of your writing skills, the quality of your finished book, and how enthusiastically you contact your readers through the media.

If you decide to go ahead, you need to consider the three phases in a book's life and the several choices you need to make within each phase:

Phase one (writing). Choose an idea that's valuable enough to develop for a group that would definitely be interested (Example: A fact-filled book on travel for the tourist market—travel agents, airlines). Decide whether to write the book yourself (harder, but cheaper) or if you need to have a co-author, a full-time editor, or a ghost writer (all easier on you, but will take more of your profits).

Phase two (publishing). You need to find a trade publisher or decide if you're going to self-publish.

Trade publishing—If you're seeking a publisher, you're really looking for another investor. You're saying to them, in effect, "Here is a money-maker. Here is a project worth the investment of your time and money because it has every chance of making a decent return. I'm willing to settle for a small royalty (5% to 8%) because I would rather you invest your money than mine. You're richer, more experienced and better organized than I am. If you agree with me, please send me a contract and an advance and I'll start the manuscript." This is equally true if you've self-published and are submitting a finished book for re-print consideration.

If they reject you, you feel disappointed, bewildered and not sure what to do next. If they agree with you and accept you, you feel overwhelmed, grateful and not sure what to do next. Unless you've been through it before, the publisher needs to help you get organized and tell you what to expect.

Self-publishing—If you're thinking of self-publish-ing, where you make all the decisions and pay for everything, it has at least three things going for it: You as the author/publisher can make four to twenty times the amount of profits any other publisher would be willing to share with you (up from 5-8% to 30-100%); your book should come out exactly the way *you* want it; and it can be started and finished in a matter of months instead of waiting a year or more after the writing is completed. A new author recently confessed, in frustration, that the manuscript he had turned in to a major trade publisher in January was scheduled to be published a year from the following August. The book you're now reading took less than six months to publish, which included research, writing, typesetting, proof corrections, printing and binding.

Phase three (publicizing). You may do nothing and depend on your publisher to do it all. You may hire a professional publicist and do whatever they arrange for you. Or, you may want to control your own publicity and get completely involved. Just remember, your time and money should be spent like a wise investor in order to obtain a reasonable return. If your book is to have any chance of making money, you need a solid marketing plan before you start. That's what this book is all about.

After reviewing all the possibilities listed in these 60 steps, you'll see that running your own publicity and personally selling your book can involve you in a very active, dynamic and exciting experience. You can literally *make* sales happen. Unfortunately, if you don't, no one else will. Not your publisher, not your distributor, no one else will do it for you. Your book might even win awards and still have disappointing sales.

Writing a best-selling book goes well beyond taking a few classes in creative writing. It involves your understanding of publishing and publicity. It demands that you take an active role in the countless details of publishing and in the relentless pursuit of publicity. Success (in this or any other activity) depends on how many things you understand and are good at, and how persistent you are at doing what's necessary.

With a strong promotional effort, you can take better control of the outcome and have the very best chance at a successful return on your investment. Furthermore, you'll live to write again and again and again.

Step 60. Review this book monthly, read the books listed in the Gray Pages section, and start a daily program of continuing self-education (including attendance at the seminars and workshops listed in the Gray Pages, whenever possible). Make your book irresistible by effectively and constantly selling its benefits to the media and your buying public— Keep this book handy. Refer to it again...and again! Develop a daily reading program that will focus your mind on the important and demanding task ahead. Be persistent. You're half way to being a successful author with a best-selling book!

Study the information in the Gray Pages section and read the books listed. Call or write the authors and editors listed and ask them questions. Every writer loves to hear from their constituency. Remember, you have the power, and the right, to make your book successful. We'll be looking for *your* name on the best-seller list.

It Can Happen!

We've reached the end of our journey together and we hope to leave you with one primary idea:

As a potentially successful author, this is your moment in the sun! Let the warm rays of public attention stimulate you. You are, for the moment, the celebrity you've always dreamed of being. There are probably some in your situation who would rather run off and hide. The great film star Greta Garbo became famous for her desire to be left alone, but then she never wrote a best-seller.

Your public, those readers who love what you write, are

waiting for you to surface. This is no time for second thoughts...*you're on!*

*It can happen! You **can** be the author of a bestseller!*

The previous chapters provide a roadmap you can follow, one step at a time until you've reached the level of success you and your book deserve. Along the way you've seen how dozens of other authors have reached sales levels they never dreamed possible by following the strategies outlined here. *It can happen!* And it can happen to you!

The magic ingredient in this process is you. You are the personification of your book...you are its voice...you are its face. Even if your book is a masterpiece, it needs you to tell the world it exists. The world is waiting for the information or entertainment contained in your book...the information or entertainment that you want to share with the world. You would never have expended the blood, sweat and tears, and all the time it takes to write a book if you weren't eager to share its contents. You've given it birth. Now it's time to nurture it and make sure it thrives.

The 60 steps included here open up doors to possibilities for you and your book. They're designed to help you make your book a bestseller. Please don't shy away from anything the world has in store for you!

Go for it! ...

Do it now! ...

Be the best you can be! ...

Be the best seller of your bestseller!

. . . *ONE LAST STEP!*

Attend seminars—Gaughen Public Relations & Book Publicity Workshops, or others listed in the Gray Pages section that are in your area, throughout your writing projects—
If you plan to be in California, the quarterly weekend workshops held in the resort community of Santa Barbara, California—Dan Poynter's on Saturday and Sunday, followed by Barbara Gaughen's on Monday—combine the beauty of a Mediterranean vacation with stimulating seminars.

These seminar leaders can also provide your writers' meetings or conventions with motivational and keynote speeches or break-out sessions on a variety of publishing and public relations topics.

To schedule your next seminar attendance, or request a speaker, contact Gaughen Public Relations—Phone: (805) 965-8482; FAX: (805) 965-6522 or call FAX-ON-DEMAND (805) 96-FAX-IT.

Book Blitz Gray Pages

Here is a world of resources in the palm of your hand. Let it serve as a reference, bibliography and guide to stacks of publications and services for the writer and self-publisher. As we go to press, we have done everything to provide the most reliable data possible. However, because the publishing industry is constantly changing, details in listings may have changed by the time you read this book.

If you have a correction or problem with the current listing, let us know. If you have found help from an additional source, let us know that too. We want to be the place writers turn to for the best information in the field.

Book Blitz Gray Pages

BONA FIDE, Part 1 ... Not Just Another Author!

The following are publications and directories that feature current authors, experts, consultants or professionals in the field of writing and literature-related services. You may wish to be included in yearly editions.

Children's Authors and Illustrators
Gale Research Company
835 Penobscot Building
Detroit, MI 48226-4094
313-961-2242/Fax: 313-961-6083
800-877-4253
Authors and illustrators of children's book and articles

Consultants and Consulting Organizations Directory
Gale Research Company
835 Penobscot Building
Detroit, MI 48226-4094
313-961-2242/Fax: 313-961-6083
800-877-4253
Consultants

Contemporary Authors
Gale Research Company
835 Penobscot Building
Detroit, MI 48226-4094
313-961-2242/Fax: 313-961-6083
800-877-4253
Major writers and book authors

Directory of American Poets and Fiction Writers
Poets & Writers
72 Spring Street
New York, NY 10012
212-226-3586/Fax 212-226-3963
Poets, novelists, short story writers

Who's Who in Advertising
Reed Reference Publishing
Marquis Who's Who
121 Chanlon Road
New Providence, NJ 07974
908-464-6800/800-521-8110
Fax (908) 665-6688
Advertising and marketing people

Who's Who in American Law
Reed Reference Publishing
Marquis Who's Who
121 Chanlon Road
New Providence, NJ 07974
908-464-6800/800-521-8110
Fax 908-665-6688
Lawyers, legal experts, etc.

Who's Who of American Women
Reed Reference Publishing
Marquis Who's Who
121 Chanlon Road
New Providence, NJ 07974
908-464-6800/800-521-8110
Fax 908-665-6688
Women leaders, women writers

Who's Who of Emerging Leaders in America
Reed Reference Publishing
Marquis Who's Who
121 Chanlon Road
New Providence, NJ 07974
908-464-6800/800-521-8110
Fax 908-665-6688
Business leaders, publishers, opinion leaders

Who's Who in Finance & Industry
Reed Reference Publishing
Marquis Who's Who
121 Chanlon Road
New Providence, NJ 07974
908-464-6800/800-521-8110
Fax 908-665-6688
Businesspeople, business writers, etc.

Who's Who in U.S. Writers, Editors & Poets
Curt Johnson, Editor
December Press
P.O. Box 302
Highland Park, IL 60035-0302
708-940-4122
The *Who's Who* of writers, editors, and poets

Yearbook of Experts, Authorities & Spokespersons
Mitchell P. Davis, Editor
Broadcast Interview Source
2233 Wisconsin Avenue NW #540
Washington, DC 20007-4104
202-333-4904/800-955-0311
A directory of experts (paid listings)

BONA FIDE, Part 2
Joining the Crowd

The following publications and directories (used by libraries, bookstores, corporations, etc.) feature current and newly marketed books and are updated every year or two.

American Reference Book Annual
Anna Grace Patterson, Editor
Libraries Unlimited
P.O. Box 6633

Englewood, CO 80155-6633
303-770-1220/Fax 303-220-8843
Reference books and directories

Association Periodicals
Gale Research Company
835 Penobscot Building
Detroit, MI 48226-4094
313-961-2242/Fax: 313-961-6083
800-877-4253
Newsletters, journals, magazines and directories

Associations Publications in Print
R.R. Bowker Company
121 Chanlon Road
New Providence, NJ 07974
908-464-6800/800-521-8110
Books published by associations

Bibliography of Books for Children
Association for Childhood Education
1105 Georgia Avenue
Wheaton, MO 20902
Fax: 301-942-3012
Children's books

Bibliographic Guide to Business and Economics
G K Hall, Library Reference
866 3rd Avenue, 20th floor
New York, NY 10022
212-702-3873/Fax 212-605-9368
Business books

The Bookfinder
American Guidance Service
4201 Woodland Rd.
P.O. Box 99 (Order Dept.)
Circle Pines, MN 55014-1796
612-786-4343/Fax 612-786-9077
Children's books

Books in Print Database
ABI Information Office
R.R. Bowker Company
121 Chanlon Road
New Providence, NJ 07974
908-464-6800/800-521-8110
Bibliographies for various areas,
including all Books in Print directories

Book Publishing Resource Guide
Marie Kiefer, Book Reviewer
Ad-Lib Publications
51-1/2 West Adams
Fairfield, IA 52556
515-472-6617/Fax: 515-472-3186
800-669-0773
Includes a bibliography of 500
directories,bibliographies and
books on printing, publishing,
marketing and publicity

Canadian Books in Print
Marian Butler, Editor
University of Toronto Press
10 St. Mary Street, Suite 700
Toronto, Ontario M4Y- 2W8
Canada
416-978-8651
Books from Canadian publishers

City & State Directories in Print
Gale Research Company
835 Penobscot Building
Detroit, MI 48226-4094
313-961-2242/Fax: 313-961-6083
800-877-4253
5,000 local directories

**Computer Publishers and
Publications**
Simba Communications Trends
213 Danbury Rd., P.O. Box 7430
Wilton, CT 06897
203- 834-0033/Fax: 203-834-1771
1200 computer publications

**Computers and
Computing Information
Resources Directory**
Gale Research Company
835 Penobscot Building
Detroit, MI 48226-4094
313-961-2242/Fax: 313-961-6083
800-877-4253
4,000 computer periodicals,
directories and books

Cumulative Book Index
H.W. Wilson Company
950 University Avenue
Bronx, NY 10452
718-588-8400/Fax 718-590-1617
All subjects

**"365 Resources to
Help You Save
Thousands of Dollars"**
Denna Millett, Editor
The Mailbox Connection
3985 North 850 East
Provo, UT 84604
801-225-7930
300 consumer & money-saving
guides

Directories in Print
Gale Research Company
835 Penobscot Building
Detroit, MI 48226-4094
313-961-2242/Fax: 313-961-6083
800-877-4253
Directories, databases

Directory of Publicity Resources
E.E.I.
66 Canal Center Plaza #200
Alexandria, VA 22314-1538
703-683-0683/Fax: 703-683-4915
Writing books, magazines, associations, etc.

Encyclopedia of Business Information Sources
Gale Research Company
835 Penobscot Building
Detroit, MI 48226-4094
313-961-2242/Fax: 313-961-6083
1,100 print and electronic sources of business information

Encyclopedia of Health Information Sources
Gale Research Company
835 Penobscot Building
Detroit, MI 48226-4094
313-961-2242/Fax: 313-961-6083
13,000 medical directories, books, publications and services

Encyclopedia of Physical Science and Engineering Information Sources
Gale Research Company
835 Penobscot Building
Detroit, MI 48226-4094
313-961-2242/Fax: 313-961-6083
13,000 physics and engineering directories, books, publications and services

Encyclopedia of Public Affairs Information Services
Gale Research Company
835 Penobscot Building
Detroit, MI 48226-4094
313-961-2242/Fax: 313-961-6083
8,000 public affairs directories, books and services

Encyclopedia of Senior Citizens Information Sources
Gale Research Company
835 Penobscot Building
Detroit, MI 48226-4094
313-961-2242/Fax: 313-961-6083

Retirement directories, books and services

Gale Directory of Publications and Broadcast Media
Gale Research Company
835 Penobscot Building
Detroit, MI 48226-4094
313-961-2242/Fax: 313-961-6083
35,000 magazines, newspapers, radio, TV and directories

Gayellow Pages
Renaissance House Publishing
P.O. Box 533, Village Station
New York, NY 10014-0292
212-674-0120
Gay bookstores, publications and resources

Guide to American Directories
Barry Klein, Editor
Todd Publications, P.O. Box 301
West Nyack, NY 10994-8503
914-358-6213/Fax: 914-358-6213
8,000 directories

Pricing Guide for Desktop Publishing Services
Brenner Information Group
13223 Black Mountain Rd. #1-430
San Diego, CA 92129
619-538-0093
Desktop publishing books

Index to Handicraft Books
University of Pittsburgh Press
127 N. Bellefield Avenue
Pittsburgh, PA 15260
412-624-4110/Fax 412-624-7380
900 craft titles

Jewish Book Annual
Paula Gottlieb, Director
Jewish Book Council of America
15 East 26th Street
New York, NY 10010-1505
212-532-4949/Fax 212-481-4174
Jewish books

Law & Legal Information Directory
Gale Research Company
835 Penobscot Building
Detroit, MI 48226-4094
313-961-2242/Fax: 313-961-6083
12,000 law assns., publications, etc.

Law Books in Print
Fay Cohen, President
Glenville Publications
75 Main Street
Dobbs Ferry, NY 10522-1601
914-693-5944/Fax 914-693-0402
Legal books

Learning AIDS
American Foundation for AIDS Research
733 3rd Avenue, 12th floor
New York, NY 10017
212-682-7440/Fax 212-682-9812
AIDS books, brochures, tapes, films

Multicultural Children's and Young Adult Literature
Cooperative Children's Book Cntr.
600 N. Park Street
Madison, WI 53706
608-263-3720/Fax 608-262-4933
250 multicultural children's titles

Notable Children's Books
Assn. for Library Svs. to Children
312-280-2163/Fax 312-280-3257

American Library Association
50 E. Huron Street
Chicago, IL 60611-2795
312-944-6780
Children's books

On Cassette
R.R. Bowker Company
121 Chanlon Road
New Providence, NJ 07974
908-464-6800/800-521-8110
22,000 spoken word audiotapes

Optical Publishing Directory
James H. Shelton, Editor
Learned Information Inc.
143 Old Marlton Pike
Medford, NJ 08055-8750
609-654-6266/Fax: 609-654-4309
CD-ROM products, including
books on CD-ROM

Paperback Books for Young People: An Annotated Guide
American Library Association
50 E. Huron Street
Chicago, IL 60611-2795
312-944-6780
Children's & young adult paperbacks

Reading Aloud with Children
The Child Study Book Committee
Bank Street College
610 West 112th Street
New York, NY 10025-1898
212-875-4400/Fax 212-875-4759
400 titles for children (to age 8)

Real Estate Books & Periodicals in Print
Real Estate Publishing Company
P.O. Box 41177
Sacramento, CA 95841-0177
916-677-3864
Real estate books

**Reference Sources
for Small and Medium-
Sized Libraries**
ALA Reference & Adult Services
American Library Association
50 E. Huron Street
Chicago, IL 60611-2795
312-944-6780
Reference books for libraries

The Serials Directory
EBSCO Publishing
P.O. Box 1943
Birmingham, AL 35201-1943
205-991-1330/Fax: 205-991-1479
800-826-3024
118,000 magazines and directories

**SIE Guide to
Business and
Investment Books**
George H. Wein, Editor
Select Information Exchange
244 West 54th St., Suite 614
New York, NY 10019
212-247-7123/Fax 212-247-7326
Business and investment books

**Small Press Record of
Books in Print**
Len Fulton, Editor
Dustbooks, P.O. Box 100
Paradise, CA 95967-0100
916-877-6110
Small press books, all subjects

Software Encyclopedia
R.R. Bowker Company
121 Chanlon Road
New Providence, NJ 07974
908-464-6800/800-521-8110
New computer software products

Standard Periodical Directory
Deborah Waithe, Senior Editor
Oxbridge Communications
150 Fifth Avenue, # 302
New York, NY 10011-4311
212-741-0231/Fax: 212-633-2938
78,000 magazines, newspapers,
newletters and directories

**Trade Directories
of the World**
Elizabeth Duffy, Editor
Croner Publications
34 Jericho Turnpike
Jericho, NY 11753
718-464-0866/Fax 516-338-4986
Business directories

**Ulrich's International
Periodicals Directory**
R.R. Bowker Company
121 Chanlon Road
New Providence, NJ 07974
908-464-6800/800-521-8110
111,600 magazines and other
periodicals, including directories

**Variety's Home
Video Directory**
Scott MacFarland, Editor
R.R. Bowker Company
121 Chanlon Road
New Providence, NJ 07974
908-464-6800/800-521-8110
Home videos

The Video Source Book
Gale Research Company
835 Penobscot Building
Detroit, MI 48226-4094
313-961-2242/Fax: 313-961-6083
800-877-4253
54,000 videos

Words on Tape
R.R. Bowker Co.
121 Chanlon Road
New Providence, NJ 07974
908-464-6800/800-521-8110

BONA FIDE, Part 3
And The Award Goes To ...

A small sampling of awards given out annually to book authors and publishers.

AMWA Medical Book Awards
Book Awards Committee
American Medical Writers Assn.
9650 Rockville Pike
Bethesda, MD 20814
301-493-0003/Fax 301-493-0005
Best medical books for physicians, health professionals and laypeople

Benjamin Franklin Awards
Jan Nathan, Director
Publishers Marketing Association
2401 Pacific Coast Highway #102
Hermosa Beach, CA 90254
310-372-2732/Fax: 310-374-3342
30 awards for independent publishers

Book Show Awards
Wadsworth Publishing
10 Davis Drive
Belmont, CA 94002
415-595-2350
7 awards for book design & production

California Writers Club
2214 Derby Street
Berkeley, CA 94705
Writing contest for unpublished material (six categories)

Children's Science-Writing Award in Physics and Astronomy
American Institute of Physics
335 East 45th Street
New York, NY 10017-3483
212-661-9404; Fax: 212-949-0473
Science book or magazine article

Denali Press Award
Andrew Hansen
American Library Association
50 E. Huron Street
Chicago, IL 60611-2795
312-944-6780, 800-545-2433
Annual award for best minority or ethnic reference book

Gold Ink Awards
Publishing & Production Executive
North American Publishing
401 N. Broad Street
Philadelphia, PA 19108-1074
215-238-5300; Fax: 215-238-5457
21 awards for production of books, catalogs, magazines, etc.

Gold Medallion Book Awards
Evangelical Christian Publishers Association
3225 South Hardy Drive
Tempe, AZ 85282
602-966-3998; Fax: 602-996-1944
20 awards for Christian books

Ernest Hemingway Award
Martha Albrand Award
Pen American Center
568 Broadway
New York, NY 10012
212-334-1660

"IACP Julia Child Cookbook Awards"
International Association of
Culinary Professionals
304 W. Liberty #201
Louisville, KY 40202
502-581-9786/Fax (502) 589-3602
Best books for food and beverage
professionals

LMP Awards
R.R. Bowker Company
121 Chanlon Road
New Providence, NJ 07974
908-464-6800/800-521-8110
10 awards

NABE Book of the Year Awards
No. Amer. Booksellers Exchange
Al Galasso, Director
International Bookmarketing Org.
P.O. Box 606
Cottage Grove, OR 97424
503-942-7455

National Jewish Book Awards
Marie Jeanniton, Coordinator
JWB, Jewish Book Council
15 East 26th Street
New York, NY 10010
212-532-4949/Fax (212) 481-4174
20 awards for Jewish-related books

NCCJ Mass Media Awards
National Conference of
Christians and Jews
71 Fifth Avenue #1100
New York, NY 10003
212-206-0006/Fax (212) 255-6177
Best book on human relations

Ozzie Awards
South Wind Publications
8340 Mission Road #106

Prairie Village, KS 66206
913-642-6611/Fax: 913-642-6676
50 categories—best design of magazines, magazine covers, newsletters, annual reports, directories and books

PIA Graphic Arts Award
Printing Industries of America
100 Dangerfield Road
Alexandria, VA 22314
703-841-8153

Pulitzer Prize
Publitzer Committee
Graduate School of Journalism
706 Journalism Hall
Columbia University
116th Street and Broadway
New York, NY 10027

The Pushcart Prize
Bill Henderson, Publisher
The Pushcart Press
P.O. Box 380
Wainscott, NY 11975
516-324-9300
Portions of books (chapter or stories)

CONNECTIONS, Part 1 Join A Book Publishing Association

A comprehensive listing of book
publishing associations in the
United States.

American Booksellers Association
560 White Plains Road
Tarrytown, NY 10591
914-631-7800/Fax: 914-631-8391
800-637-0037

American Library Association
50 East Huron Street
Chicago. IL 60611
312-944-6780

Association of American Publishers
220 East 23rd Street
New York, NY 10010-4686
212-689-8920/Fax: 212-696-0131
Most larger publishers belong

Association of American University Presses
Peter Grenquist, Exec. Director
584 Broadway #410
New York, NY 10012-3229
212-941-6610/Fax 212-941-6618
100 university presses

Association of Canadian Publishers
260 King Street East
Toronto, ON M5A 1K3, Canada

Bay Area Publisher Network
Patrick Fanning
New Harbinger Press
5674 Shattuck Avenue
Oakland, CA 94609
510-652-0215
San Francisco area publishers

Best-Seller Books
Gaughen Public Relations
226 East Canon Perdido, Suite B1
Santa Barbara, CA 93101
805-965-8482/Fax: 805-965-6522
FAX-ON-DEMAND (805) 96-FAX IT
Books and other materials on
book publicity

Book Publicists of Southern California
Irwin Zucker, Founder/President

6464 Sunset Boulevard #580
Hollywood, CA 90028-8007
213-461-3921/Fax: 213-461-0917
1200 members (many authors and
publicists)

Book Publishers of Texas
Pam Lange, Editor
Publisher Digest Newsletter
3404 S. Ravina Drive
Dallas, TX 75233
214-330-9795/Fax: 214-330-9795

Calendar Marketing Association
Maria Tuthill, Director
American Custom Publishing
621 E. Park Avenue
Libertyville, IL 60048
708-816-8660/Fax: 708-816-8662
800-828-8225

California Writers Club
2214 Derby Street
Berkeley, CA 94705

Canadian Book Centre
Mary Neuitt, Director
For Immediate Release Newsletter
M4Y-IL5
2 Glouster St., Suite 301
Toronto, Ontario M5A 1K3
Canada
416-413-4930/Fax: 416-361-0643
Canadian book publishing center

Catholic Press Association
119 North Park Avenue
Rockville Center, NY 11570
516-766-3400

Children's Book Council
568 Broadway, New York, NY 10012
212-996-1990
70 companies

Christian Booksellers Association
P.O. Box 200
Colorado Springs, CO 80901
719-576-7880

COSMEP
The International Association of Independent Publishers
Richard Morris, Director
P.O.Box 420703
San Francisco, CA 94142-0703
415-922-9490/Fax: 922-5566
1300 members

Direct Marketing Association
6 East 43rd Street
New York, NY 10017
212-768-7277

Educational Press Association
Donald Stoll, Executive Director
Rowan Collge of NY
201 Mullica Hill Road
Glassboro, NJ 08028
609-863-7349/Fax: 609-863-5012
Educational magazine, book printers

Evangelical Christian Publishers Association
Doug Ross, Director
3225 So. Hardy Dr., Suite 101
Tempe, AZ 85282
602-966-3998/Fax: 602-966-1944
60 companies

Greeting Card Association
1200 G St., N.W., Suite 760
Washington, DC 20005
202-393-1778

The Independent Publishers Guide
Rosemary Pettit, Bulletin Editor

147-149 Gloucester Terrace
London W2 6DX England
01-723-7328

Independent Publishers' Guild
52 Chepstow Road
London W2, Great Britain

Jewish Book Council of America
Paula Gribetz Gottlieb, Director
15 East 26th Street
New York, NY 10010-1505
212-532-4949
Bookstores, publishers and centers

Maine Writers & Publishers Alliance
12 Pleasant Street
Brunswick, ME 04011-1513
207-729-6333

Marin Small Publishers Assn.
P.O. Box E
Corte Madera, CA 994937
415-454-1771

Michigan Publishers Association
Sherry Wells
Lawells Publishing, P.O. Box 1338
Royal Oak, MI 48068-1338
313-543-5297

Mid-America Publishers Assn.
P.O. Box 30242
Lincoln, NE 68503-0242
402-466-9665/Fax: 402-466-9093

Minnesota Publishers' Roundtable
Kathy Grooms, President
Cy De Cosse Co.
5900 Green Oak Drive
Minneapolis, MN 55343
612-378-9076

Multicultural Publishers Exchange
Charles Taylor, Director
2215 Atwood Avenue
P.O. Box 9869
Madison, WI 53715
608-244-5633/Fax; 608-244-3255

New Age Publishing and Retailing Alliance
P.O. Box 9
Eastsound, WA 98245
206-376-2702/Fax: 206-376-2704

New Hampshire Writers and Publishers
P.O. Box 150
Portsmouth, NH 03802-0150
603-430-9475

North American Bookdealers Exchange
Al Galasso, Director
P.O. Box 606
Cottage Grove, OR 07424
503-942-7455

Northwest Association of Book Publishers
P.O. Box 633
Maryhurst, OR 97036
503-293-8583

Publishers Assn. of South
Holly Burns
P.O. Box 43533
Birmingham, AL 36243
205-967-4387

Publishers Marketing Assn.
Jan Nathan, Director
2401 Pacific Coast Highway #102
Hermosa Beach, CA 90254
310-372-2732/Fax: 310-374-3342

Publishers' Publicity Association
Helen Atwan, Secretary
Farrar, Straus and Giroux
19 Union Square West
New York, NY 10003
212-741-6920
A network of N Y area book publicists

Religious Publishing Group
Patti Gatzke
c/o Orbis Books, Walsh Building
Maryknoll, NY 10545
914-941-7636

Rocky Mountain Book Publishers
Alan Stark, Executive Director
2920 Pearl Street, 2nd Floor
Boulder, CO 80301
303-447-2320/Fax: 303-447-9710

Scottish Publishers' Association
25A SW Thistle Street Lane
Edinburgh EH2 1EW Scotland
031-225-5795; Fax: 031-220-0377

Small Press Action Network
Normal Art Society
P.O. Box 65746, Station F
Vancouver British Columbia V5N 5KY
Canada

Small Press Group of Britain
John Nicholson, Editor
Small Press Monthly
P.O. Box 556
London SE5 ORL England
0234-211606

Society for Scholarly Publishing
10200 West 44th Avenue #304
Wheat Ridge, CO 80033
303-422-3914

Special Interest Video Association CIVA
Paul Cervatt, President
10 Byington Place
Norwalk, CT 06850
303-850-0688
Special interest video producers

Vermont Publishers Association
Margo Baldwin, President
Chelsea Green Publishing Company
Route 113, P.O. Box 130
Post Mills, VT 05058
802-333-9073

Wisconsin Authors & Publishers Association
Arnold Grummer, President
1916 Drew Street
Appleton, WI 54911

CONNECTIONS, Part 2
Booksellers Associations

You never know what a good connection will provide and these are some of the best!

American Booksellers Association
560 White Plains Road
Tarrytown, NY 10591
914-631-7800/Fax: 914-631-8391
800-637-0037

Assn. of Booksellers for Children
Caron Chapman
4412 Chowen Ave., So. #303
Minneapolis, MN 55410
612-926-6650

Booksellers Association of Georgia
Rupret Le Craw, President
Oxford Books
360 Pharr Road
Atlanta, GA 30305
404-364-2700/Fax: 404-262-9975

Christian Booksellers Association
P.O. Box 200
Colorado Springs, CO 80901
719-576-7880

Great Lakes Booksellers Association
Jim Dana, Director
509 LaFayette Dtreet
Grand Haven, MI 49417
800-745-2460/Fax: 616-842-0051

Mid-Atlantic Booksellers Association
Robin's Bookstore
108 South 13th Street
Philadelphia, PA 19017
215-735-9599

Midwest Booksellers Association
Phil Black, President
The Bookworm
120 Regency Parkway
Omaha, NE 68114
402-392-2877/Fax: 402-392-0112

Mountain & Plains Booksellers Association
805 La Porte
Fort Collins, CO 80521
303-484-5856

National Association of College Stores
528 E. Lorain Street, P.O. Box 58
Oberlin, OH 44074-0058
216-775-7777/Fax: 216-775-4769

New England Booksellers Association
Wayne Drugan, Director
45 Newbury Street #506
Boston, MA 02116
617-421-9340

New Orleans and Gulf Coast Booksellers Association
1 Shell Square, 119 Concourse
New Orleans, LA 70139
504-525-1846

New York Regional Booksellers Association
151 East 26th Street #2A
New York, NY 10010
212-725-0054

Northern California Booksellers Association
Elizabeth Bogner, Coordinator
2141 Kitridge Street #1
Berkeley, CA 94704
415-644-3666

Oklahoma Independent Booksellers Association
Yorktown Bookstore
2046 Utica Square
Tulsa, OK 74114
918-747-2539

San Diego Booksellers Assn.
Butler and Mayes Booksellers
5650 Riley Street
San Diego, CA 92110
619-291-6399

South Central Booksellers Assn.
Square Books
115-1/2 S. Lamar
P.O. Box 993
Oxford, MS 38655
601-236-2262

Southeast Booksellers Assn.
Lois Mendenhall, President
The Happy Bookseller
4525 Forest Drive
Columbia, SC 29206
803-787-1503

Southern California Booksellers Association
Pacific Bookstore
11755 Wilshire Boulevard #40
Los Angeles, CA 90025
213-312-1819

Southwest Booksellers Association
Eidos Productions
3404 S. Ravina Drive
Dallas, TX 75233
214-330-9795

Texas Association of Booksellers for Children (TABC)
Toad Hall, 3918 Far West Blvd.
Austin, TX 78731
512-345-8637

Upper Midwest Booksellers Association
4018 West 65th St.
Minneapolisl, MN 55435-1727
612-934-7422/612-293-0162

ON THE LOOKOUT, Part 1
Who Does What, Now That I've Written It

The directories listed below consist of publishers and publishing-related services available.

AAUP Directory
Peter Grenquist, Executive Director
Association of American
University Presses
584 Broadway #410
New York, NY 10012-3229
212-941-6610/Fax 212-941-6618

ABA Book Buyer's Handbook
Daniel Cullen, Editor
560 White Plains Rd.
Tarrytown, NY 10591
914-631-7800/Fax 914-631-8391
Publisher's terms for bookstore buyers

Artist's Market
Writer's Digest Books
1507 Dana Avenue
Cincinnati, OH 45207
513-531-2222/Fax: 513-531-4744
800-543-4644
Book publishers using artists

AV Market Place
Reed Reference Publishers
121 Chanlon Road
New Providence, NJ 07974
908-464-6800/800-521-8110

Black Resource Guide
R. Benjamin Johnson, Editor
501 Oneida Place NW
Washington, DC 20011
202-291-4373
Listings including book publishers

Book Trade in Canada
Ampersand Communications Svs.
RR #1 Caledon, Ontario L0N 1C0
Canada
519-927-3321
Publishers, bookstores

Business Organizations, Agencies & Publications Directory
Gale Research Company
835 Penobscot Building
Detroit, MI 48226-4094
313-961-2242/Fax: 313-961-6083
24,000 information services and publications

California Publishing Marketplace
Steve & Meera Lester, owners
Writer's Connection
275 Saratoga Avenue,
Suite 103
Santa Clara, CA 95050
408-554-2090/Fax 408-554-2099
California newspapers, magazines and book publishers

Canadian Publishers Directory
Key Publishers
59 E. Front Street
Toronto, Ontario M5E 1B3
Canada
416-364-3333
Canada publishers

Cassell's Directory
P.O. Box C-831
Rutherford, NY 07070
212-799-1822/Fax 212-779-1834
1,100 British Commonwealth book publishers

**Children's Media
Market Place**
Margo Hart, Dir. of Mkting &
Edit.
Neal-Schuman Publications
100 Varick Street
New York, NY 10013-2918
212-925-8650/Fax 212-219-8916
Children's publishers, clubs, stores,etc.

Children's Writer's Market
F&W Publications
Writer's Digest Books
1507 Dana Avenue
Cincinnati, OH 45207
513-531-2222/Fax: 513-4744
Children's publishers & magazines

Christian Writers Market Guide
Sally Stuart, Editor
Joy Publishing
P.O. Box 827
San Juan Capistrano, CA 92675
714-493-4552/Fax 714-493-6552
Religious book & magazine publishers

Directory of Poetry Publishers
Len Fulton, Publisher
Dustbooks, P.O.Box 100
Paradise, CA 95967-0100
916-877-6110/Fax: 916-877-0222
800-477-6110
Poetry book & magazine publishers

Directory of Publishing
The Oryx Press
4041 N. Central
Phoenix, AZ 85012
602-265-2651/Fax: 602-265-6250
800-279-ORYX

**Directory of Small Magazine/
Press Editors & Publishers**
Len Fulton, Editor
Dustbooks, P.O. Box 100

Paradise, CA 95967-0100
916-877-6110/Fax: 916-877-0222
800-477-6110
Small press publishers

**Directory of Texas Markets for
Writers and PR Professionals**
Texas Free-Lance Writers Associa-
tion (plus Georgia,Florida)
Dana Cassell, Director
Maple Ridge Road
North Sandwich, NH 03259
603-284-6367/Fax 603-284-6648
Texas, Georgia and Florida markets for
writers, including book publishers

Directory of Women's Media
Natl. Council for Research on Women
530 Broadway, 10th Floor
New York, NY 10021
212-570-5001
Women's magazines, bookstores, radio
stations, book pub- lishers& other
women's media groups

Guide to Bay Area Book Publishers
San Francisco Review of Books
1117 Geary Street
San Francisco, CA 94109-6845
415-771-1252

Hunter House, Inc.
2200 Central Ave., Suite 202
Alameda, CA 91711
501-865-5282/Fax: 501-865-4292
Women's health books, Amnesty Intl.

**International Directory of
Children's Literature**
George Kurian Reference Books
P.O. Box 519
Baldwin Place, NY 10505-0519
914-962-3287
Children's book clubs, bookstores,
publishers, etc.

International Directory of Little Magazines and Small Presses
Len Fulton, Editor
Dustbooks
P.O. Box 100
Paradise, CA 95967-0100
916-877-6110/Fax: 916-877-0222
800-477-6110
Small press book and magazine publishers

International Literary Market Place
R.R. Bowker Company
121 Chanlon Road
New Providence, NJ 07974
908-464-6800/800-521-8110
International publishers

Literary Market Place
R.R. Bowker Company
121 Chanlon Road
New Providence, NJ 07974
908-464-6800/800-521-8110
Publishers, suppliers, etc.

NACS Book Buyer's Manual
Elizabeth Livermore, Editor
National Assn. of College Stores
500 E. Lorain Street
Oberlin, OH 44074-0058
216-775-7777/Fax 216-775-4769
Publisher's terms for college books

New Age Directory
Survival Foundation
P.O. Box 64
Woodstock Valley, CT 06282
Fax 203-974-2440
New age centers, publishers, etc.

Novel and Short Story Writer's Market
Writer's Digest Books

F&W Publications
1507 Dana Avenue
Cincinnati, OH 45207
513-531-2222/Fax 513-531-4744
Fiction book publishers

Photographer's Market
Writer's Digest Books
F&W Publications
1507 Dana Avenue
Cincinnati, OH 45207
513-531-2222/Fax 513-531-4744
Lists users of photographers work

Poet's Market
Judson Jerome, Editor
P.O. Box 740
Yellow Springs, OH 45387
513-767-9438/Fax: 513-531-4744
Poetry book & magazine publishers

Running Press
Nancy Steele, Editor
125 South 22nd Street
Philadelphia, PA 19103-4399
215-567-5080; Fax: 215-568-2919
Crosswords, poetry, mini-books, classics, coffeetable books

Policies of Publishers: A Handbook for Order Librarians
Scarecrow Press
52 Liberty Street
P.O. Box 4167
Metuchen, NJ 08840
908-548-8600/Fax 908-548-5767
Publishers' terms for libraries

Publishers' Catalogs Annual
Chadwyck-Healey
Megan Schneider, Editor
1101 King Street, Suite 380
Alexandria, VA 22314
703-683-4890/Fax 703-683-7589
Publishers' catalogs on microfilm

Publishers Directory
Gale Research Company
835 Penobscot Bldg.
Detroit, MI 48226-4094
313-961-2242; Fax: 313-961-6083
800-877-4253
Book publishers and others

Publishers, Distributors and Wholesalers of the U.S.
R.R. Bowker Company
121 Chanlon Road
New Providence, NJ 07974
908-464-6800/800-521-8110
49,000 publishers and wholesalers

Publishers Trade List Annual
R.R. Bowker Company
121 Chanlon Road
New Providence, NJ 07974
908-464-6800/800-521-8110
Book publishers catalog (paid ads)

Selling to Other Educational Markets
Jane Williams, Author/Editor
Bluestocking Press
P.O. Box 1014
Placerville, CA 95667
916-621-1123
Books, newsletters and other resources for those selling to alternative and home education markets

Source Directory
364 Lakeside Drive
Foster City, CA 94404
800-321-6388
Sources of business information

Who's Who in African Heritage Book Publishing
Mwalimu Mwadilifu, President
P.O. Box 15004, Great Bridge Station

Chesepeake, VA 23320
804-547-5542
A black literary marketplace

Writer's Guide to Texas Markets
Attn: Editor
University of North Texas Press
P.O. Box 13856
Denton, TX 76203-6856
817-565-2142
Texas book and magazine publishers

Writer's Market
F&W Publications
Writer's Digest Books
1507 Dana Avenue
Cincinnati, OH 45207
513-531-2222/Fax 513-531-4744
800-543-4644
Book and magazine publishers

Writer's Northwest Handbook
Dennis Stovall, Publ.
Linny Stoval, Editor
Media Weavers
24450 N.W. Hansen Road
Hillsboro, OR 97124
503-621-3911
Pacific Northwest book and magazine publishers

Writers Resource Guide / Seattle
William R. Griffin, Publisher
Writers Publishing Service
1512 Western Avenue
Seattle, WA 98101
206-467-6735
Seattle writer's associations, newsletters, markets, etc.

BEEN THERE, DONE THAT, Part 1
Promotion

Book BLITZ, Getting Your Book in the News by Barbara Gaughen and Ernest Weckbaugh 60 steps for successfully promoting your book. How to get your name in the papers, your voice on the radio and your face on television. Includes "Gray Pages"—42-page resources directory—just like a publicist on your bookshelf. ISBN 1-881474-02-X, softcover, 5-1/2 x 8-1/2, 268 pages, $12.95

Book Fairs, An Exhibiting Guide for Publishers by Dan Poynter. Inside tips on how to operate a booth at a book fair. Required reading for first time exhibitors and valuable reminder/checklist for the seasoned veteran. ISBN 0-915516-43-8, softcover, 5-1/2 x 8-1/2, 96 pages, $7.95

Copy Writer's Handbook, A Practical Guide for Advertising and Promotion of Specialized, Scholarly Books and Journals by Nat G. Bodian. Creating effective copy for ads, direct mail, book covers, headline writing, testimonials and more. Hundreds of examples and case histories. ISBN 0-89495-039-8, softcover, 6-3/4 x 10-1/2, 277 pages, $19.95

How to Get Publicity and Make the Most of It Once You've Got It by William Parkhurst. Techniques for booking and conducting radio, television and print interviews, writing news releases, designing press kits and more. No one wants to be surprised in an interview. ISBN 0-8129-1161-X, hardcover, 6 x 8-1/2, 245 pages, $14.95

Publicity for Books and Authors by Peggy Glenn shows authors and publicists how to get free and effective publicity for their books. Her own experiences on TV talk shows, radio, magazine and newspaper interviews and what worked, what didn't and why. Many examples and ideas. ISBN 0-936930-91-8, softcover, 8-1/2 x 11, 182 pages, $12.95

The Publicity Manual by Kate Kelly. Increase the visibility of your books through free publicity in newspapers, magazines, newsletters, trade journals, and on radio and television. A complete, inexpensive course with examples. ISBN 0-9603740-1-9, softcover, 8-1/2 x 11, 243 pages, $19.95

The Unabashed Self-Promoter's Guide by Jeffrey Lant, Ph.D. He is a master at obtaining free publicity and then pyramiding it to promote more publicity. How to generate articles about yourself and your book, how to arrange and handle print and radio/TV interviews. Great promotional ideas, samples and contracts. ISBN 0-940374-06-4, softcover,

8-1/2 x 11, 366 pages, $29.95

Words That Sell by Richard Bayan. A thesaurus for promoting products, services and ideas. A short, valuable course, this unusual *advertising copy simulator* lists synonyms for the words you need to use.
ISBN 0-87280-150-0, softcover, 5-1/2 x 8-3/4, 128 pages, $9.95

BEEN THERE, DONE THAT, Part 2 Marketing

Gale Directory of Publications & Broadcast Media (see p. 209)

Guerrilla Marketing Attack, New Strategies, Tactics & Weapons for Winning Big Profits from Your Small Business by Jay Conrad Levinson. The advanced course on direct marketing, zip code inserts, TV shopping networks, and much more. Filled with tips, personal insights and real-life examples.
ISBN 0-395-50220-9, softcover, 6 x 9, 224 pages, $8.95

Guerrilla Marketing, Secrets for Making Big Profits from Your Small Business by Jay Conrad Levinson. How to get the most from telemarketing, classified ads, Yellow Pages, newspapers, radio, TV, brochures, direct mail, seminars and more. A game plan to cut costs, increase profits and give you a winning edge.
ISBN 0-395-38314-5, softcover,

6 x 9, 226 pages, $8.95

Money Making Marketing by Jeffrey Lant. Find the people who need what you're selling, make them buy, then turn them into steady customers. Effective and inexpensive marketing techniques.
ISBN 0-940374-12-9, softcover, 8-1/2 x 11, 285 pages, $29.95

1001 Ways to Market Your Books by John Kremer. Creative and informative manual on book marketing from Kremer's detailed research and hard-earned experience. Advertising, promotion, distribution, bookstores, book design, libraries and spinoffs.
ISBN 0-912411-19-8, softcover, 6 x 9, 384 pages, $14.95

The Publisher's Direct Mail Handbook by Nat Bodian. The last word on direct mail marketing. Full of facts and figures, easy and fun to read. A summary of all other books on direct mail advertising, a vertible degree in book marketing.
ISBN 0-89495-079-7, hardcover, 7 x 10-1/2, 256 pages, $39.95

Selling to Catalog Houses by Ron Playle. How to sell books to mail order catalog houses. Contains sample letters, pricing guidelines and many addresses.
Softcover, 8-1/2 x 11, 48 pages, $8.95

Specialty Booksellers Directory by John Kremer. This valuable reference lists over 2100 bookstores by specialty. Mail just to those specializing in your type of book, not every bookstore.
ISBN 0-912411-16-3, softcover,

Successful Direct Marketing Methods (New Expanded Edition) by Bob Stone. The *Bible* for marketing your book—direct mail, magazines, newspapers and broadcasting directly to your reader at the least possible cost. . This book shows how smaller publishers of narrow-market books have an advantage over the big New York publishers.
ISBN 0-87251-040-9, hardcover, 7-1/2 x 9-1/2, 575 pages, $29.95

BEEN THERE, DONE THAT, Part 3
Taking Care of Business

Building a Mail Order Business by William A. Cohen. If you use the Postal Service or UPS, you're in the mail order business. From start-up to running a huge mail order business, Cohen covers it all.
ISBN 0-471-81062-2, hardcover, 6-1/2 x 9-1/4, 565 pages, $27.95

A Business Guide to Copyright Law by Woody Young. His book explains copyright law, how much research you may legally use and how to protect your work from others. It covers fair use, permissions, licensing, foreign protection, registration procedures and much more. Glossary, examples of forms.
ISBN 0-939513-51-X, softcover, 8-1/2 x 11, 98 pages, $9.95

The Business Planning Guide, Creating a Plan for Success in Your Own Business by David H. Bangs. How to set up a business, organize, get your paperwork together, register in the proper places and borrow money.
ISBN 0-936894-10-5, softcover, 8-1/2 x 11, 149 pages, $16.95

Empire Building by Gordon Burgett. In 15 steps, Burgett shows you how to define goals, evaluate needs and resources, select your core topic, research it, identify the appropriate means of idea dissemination, create action paths and find markets...how to turn your writing into books, articles, newsletters, speeches, classes, seminars, workshops and consulting.
ISBN 0-910167-02-8, softcover, 6 x 9, 192 pages, $12.95

Financial Feasibility in Book Publishing by Robert Follett presents a step-by-step method for evaluating the financial future of new book projects. Worksheets, guidelines, projection methods, rules of thumb and estimating methods (with explanations) help you decide whether your book will make money.
ISBN 0-931712-07-6, softcover, 8-1/2 x 11, 64 pages, $12.95

How to Become a Successful Consultant in Your Own Field by Hubert Bermont. Capitalize on your years of experience by opening a new profit center. How to get started, how to find clients, what to charge, how to handle clients. Proposal and report writing,
ISBN 0-930686-22-5, softcover, 7 x 10, 147 pages, $29.95

Publishing Agreements by Charles Clark. Sample book contracts, with explanations of each paragraph, ranging from those for general books to academic books, to paperback rights, translator agreements, and a book club contract. New third revision (after being out of print 8 months). ISBN 0-941533-56-5, hardcover, 6 x 9, 238 pages, $29.95

BEEN THERE, DONE THAT, Part 4 Publishing

Book Publishing, A Basic Introduction by John P. Dessauer. An inside look at the publishing industry—how books are created, manufactured, marketed, stored, delivered...how publishers finance, plan and manage. ISBN 0—8264-0446-4, hardcover, 5-1/2 x 8-1/2, 246 pages, $24.95

Directory of Book, Catalog and Magazine Printers (New, Expanded Fourth Edition) by John Kremer. The capabilities of over 900 specialty printers—addresses, price comparisons and general comments. Explains a request for quotation and each element of the bid. Just being able to compare printers makes this book a valuable reference. ISBN 0-912411-13-9, softcover, 5-1/2 x 8-1/2, 240 pages, $14.95

How to Get Happily Published by Judith Appelbaum. Learn how the publishing industry works—write, find a publisher, locate an agent, self-publish—from one with years of experience in New York publishing houses. A gold mine of publishing information with a lengthy resource section. All new third edition. ISBN 0-06-015838-7, hardcover, 6 x 8-1/2, 304 pages, $18.95

The Self-Publishing Manual, How to Write, Print & Sell Your Own Book by Dan Poynter. A complete course in writing, publishing, marketing, promoting and distributing books. It takes the reader step-by-step from idea through manuscript, printing, detailed book marketing techniques, and sales—an in-depth study of the book publishing industry. ISBN 0-915516-37-3, softcover, 5-1/2 x 8-1/2, 352 pages, $14.95

BEEN THERE, DONE THAT, Part 5 Fiction, Fantasy, Facts

Courses, conferences and seminars. There are many educational programs of interest to publishers and some of the most important are listed here. For more, see *Literary Market Place.*

Book Public Relations Seminars (Quarterly in Santa Barbara) Barbara Gaughen 226 E. Canon Perdido, Suite B1 Santa Barbara, CA 93101 805-965-8482/Fax: 805-965-6522 FAX-ON-DEMAND 805-96-FAX-IT

Chicago Book Clinic
111 E. Wacker Drive
Chicago, IL 60601
312-946-1700

New York University's Summer Publishing Institute
School of Continuing Education
Center for Publishing
48 Cooper Square
New York, NY 10211-0152
212-998-7080

Publishing Institute
University of Denver
2075 South University, #D-114
Denver, CO 80210

Publishing Program
University of Chicago
Office of Continuing Education
5835 South Kimbark Avenue
Chicago, IL 60637
312-702-1234

Santa Barbara Publishing Workshops
Dan Poynter
P.O. Box 4232
Santa Barbara,
CA 93140-4232
805-968-7277
FAX-ON-DEMAND: 805-968-8947

Stanford Conference on Book Publishing
Stanford Alumni Association
Bowman Alumni House
Stanford, CA 93405

WHAT'S THE SCORE?
Book Reviewers

About Books
50 East Huron Street, ALA
Chicago, IL 60611

American Book Review
P.O. Box 188, Cooper Station
New York, NY 10003

Authors & Books
1272 Prospect Avenue
Brooklyn, NY 11215

John Barkham Reviews
27 East 65th Street
New York, NY 10021

Bloomsbury Review
1028 Bannock Street
Denver, CO 80204
303-892-0620/Fax: 303-892-5620

Book List
American Library Association
50 E. Huron Street
Chicago, IL 60611
312-944-6780/Fax: 312-222-3143

Book Report
4200 River Road NW
Washington, DC 20016

Book Talk
8632 Horacio Place NE
Albuquerque, NM 87111

Book Talks
885 North Easton Road #6A3
Glenside, PA 19038

Bookwatch
166 Miramar Avenue
San Francisco, CA 94112

Book World
P.O. Box 107, Macon, MS 39341

Chicago Tribune Books
435 N. Michigan Avenue, Rm. 400
Chicago, IL 60611-4022
312-222-3232/Fax: 312-222-3143

Choice
100 Riverview Center
Middletown, CT 06457
203-347-6933/Fax: 203-346-8586

Fine Press Syndicate
P.O. Box 1383
New York, NY 10019

Horn Book Magazine
14 Beacon Street
Boston, MA 02108
617-227-1555

Kirkus Reviews
200 Park Avenue South #1118
New York, NY 10003-1543
212-777-4554

King Features Syndicate
235 East 45th Street
New York, NY 10017

Library Journal
249 West 17th Street
New York, NY 10011
212-463-6816/Fax: 212-242-6987

Library Talk
Linworth Publishing Company
480 E. Wilson Bridge Road #L
Worthington, OH 43085-2373
614-436-7107/Fax: 614-436-9490

Literary Lantern
418 Whitehead Circle
Chapel Hill, NC 27514

Los Angeles Review of Books
1005 Pruitt Drive
Redondo Beach, CA 90278

New Pages
4426 South Belsay Road
Grand Blanc, MI 48439

New York Review of Books
250 West 57th Street
New York, NY 10107-0001

New York Times Book Review
229 West 43rd Street
New York, NY 10036

Rainbo Electronic Reviews
8 Duran Court
Pacific, CA 94044

Reference & Research Book News
5606 NE Hassalo Street
Portland, OR 97213

Reviewing Books
709 South Irving Avenue
Scranton, PA 18505

San Francisco Review of Books
P.O. Box 33-0090
San Francisco, CA 94133

Small Press Review
P.O. Box 100
Paradise, CA 95967

Sun Features
Joyce Lain Kennedy
2382-K Camino Vida Roble
Carlsbad, CA 92009
Career books

United Features
200 Park Avenue
New York, NY 10166

United Press International
220 East 42nd Street
New York, NY 10017

**United Press International
Book Reviews**
1400 Eye Street NW
Washington, DC 20005

SEND FOR IT
Book Clubs

John Kremer's *Book Marketing
Opportunities: A Directory* has an
extensive list of book clubs noting
areas of specialization. Here are
some random examples . . .

Book-Of-The-Month Club
485 Lexington Avenue
New York, NY 10017

The Christian Bookshelf
40 Overlook Drive
Chappaqua, NY 10514

The Computer Book Store
TAB Books, Inc.
Blue Ridge Summit, PA 17214

The Doubleday Book Club
245 Park Avenue
New York, NY 10167

Get Rich Book Club
The Putter Building, 7 Putter Lane
Middle Island, NY 11953-0102

Literary Guild of America
245 Park Avenue
New York, NY 10167

MacMillan Book Clubs, Inc.
866 3rd Avenue
New York, NY 10022

Self-Sufficiency Book Club
Sub of Rodale Press, Inc.
33 East Minor Street
Emmaus, PA 18049

Small Press Book Club
Box 100, Paradise, CA 95969
(Especially appropriate for some
self-published titles, because they
concentrate solely on small
presses)

**Thoughtful Reader's
Book Society**
P.O. Box 19207
Portland, OR 97219

Watson-Guptill Book Club
1515 Broadway
New York, NY 10036

SELL IT PIECEMEAL
Selected Serial and
Excerpt Rights Buyers

Both *Writer's Market* and *Book
Marketing Opportunities: A
Directory* are good places to
prospect for possible serial rights
sales. This list includes many of
the major markets, but several
others exist...

Americana
29 W. 38th St., New York, NY 10018

American Heritage
60 Fifth Ave., New York, NY 10011

Army Magazine
2425 Wilson Boulevard
Arlington, VA 22201

Catholic Digest
Box 43090, St. Paul's Square
St. Paul, MN 55164

Chevron U.S.A. Magazine
P.O. Box 6227, San Jose, CA 95150

Cosmopolitan
224 W. 57th St., New York, NY 10019

Esquire
2 Park Avenue #1405
New York, NY 10016

Essence Magazine
1500 Broadway, New York, NY 10036

STACKS OF SALES
Large Library Systems

You can rent specialized library mailing lists from the R.R. Bowker Company (Address your query to the acquisition librarian for your specific type of book, e.g., Acquisitions Librarian, Fiction or Acquisitions Librarian, Sports, etc.) Here are a few library districts that purchase large quantities of books . . .

Atlanta Public Library
10 Pryor Street, SW
Atlanta, GA 30303

Buffalo & Erie County Public Library System
Lafayette Square
Buffalo, NY 14203

Chicago Public Library
425 North Michigan Avenue
Chicago, IL 60611

Cayuhoga County Public Library
4510 Memphis Avenue
Cleveland, OH 44144

Denver Public Library
1357 Broadway
Denver, CO 80203

Free Library of Philadelphia
Logan Square
Philadelphia, PA 19103

Houston Public Library
500 McKinney Avenue
Houston, TX 77002

Los Angeles Public Library
361 South Anderson Street
Los Angeles, CA 90033

Nassau Library System
900 Jerusalem Avenue
Uniondale, NY 11553

New York Public Library
8 East 40th Street
New York, NY 10016

San Diego County Library
555 Overland Avenue, Bldg. 15
San Diego, CA 92123

San Diego Public Library
820 "E" St., San Diego, CA 92101

USEFUL STUFF, Part 1
Brochures

Brochures on books of interest to publishers are available from the following:

R.R. Bowker Catalog
Reeds Reference Publishing
121 Chanlon Road
New Providence, NJ 07974

Direct Marketing Association
6 East 43rd Street
New York, NY 10017

Dustbooks
P.O. Box 100
Paradise, CA 95967-0100

Gale Research Company
835 Penobscot Bldg.
Detroit, MI 48226-4094

Publisher's Bookshelf
P.O. Box 4232
Santa Barbara, CA 93140-4232
FAX-ON-DEMAND (805) 968-8947

Ross Book Service
P.O. Box 12093-P
Seminary, Alexandria, VA 22304

Towers Book Store
P.O. Box 2038-P
Vancouver, WA 98661

Writer's Digest Books
1507 Dana Avenue
Cincinnati, OH 45207

The Writer, Inc.
120 Boylston Street
Boston, MA 02116

USEFUL STUFF, Part 2
Reference Books

Reference books and directories may be used and previewed at the reference desk in your public library. Write to the publishers for ordering details.

•**From** *About Books*
Communication Creativity
Tom & Marilyn Ross
P.O. Box 909
425 Cedar Street
Buena Vista, CO 81211

The Complete Guide to Self-Publishing

•**From R.R. Bowker**
Reed Reference Publishing
121 Chanlon Road
New Providence, NJ 07974

American Book Trade Directory
Lists 24,000 booksellers, wholesalers.

American Library Directory
Lists 30,000 U.S. and Canadian libraries.

Books in Print
Lists all books currently available by subject, title and author. Annual.

Forthcoming Books
Lists all books that will appear in the next edition of *Books in Print*.

International Book Trade Directory
Lists 30,000 booksellers in 170 coun- tries that handle U.S. publications.

International Literary Market Place
Lists sources outside U.S. & Canada.

International Publishers Imprints, Agents and Distributors Directory

Irregular Serials and Annuals

Literary Market Place—
Lists agents, artists, associations, book clubs, reviewers, publishers, distributors, magazines, newspapers, news services, radio and TV and many other services. Annual.

Publisher's Trade List Annual
A compilation of 1,500 publishers' catalogs.

Publishers of the United States
A directory.

Translation and Translators: An International Directory and Guide

Ulrich's International Periodicals Directory
Lists magazines

•From Dustbooks
P.O. Box 100
Paradise, CA 95967

Directory of Small Magazine/Press Editors

International Directory of Magazines and Small Presses
A comprehensive listing of smaller publishers.

Publishers International Yearbook

Small Press Record of Books in Print

•From Editor and Publisher
11 West 19th Street
New York, NY 10011

Directory of Syndicated Features

International Yearbook

Market Guide

•From Gale Research Company
835 Penobscot Bldg.
Detroit, MI 48226-4094
Send for catalog

Association Periodicals

Business, Organizations, Agencies and Publications Directory

Contemporary Authors

Directories in Print

Directory of Publications
(Formerly Ayer Directory of Publications)

Directory of Special Libraries

Encyclopedia of Associations

International Directories in Print

Newsletters in Print

Publishers Directory

Standard Periodical Directory
(Oxbridge)

•**From B. Klein Publications**
P.O. Box 8503
Coral Springs, FL 33075

Directory of Mailing List Houses

Guide to American Directories

Mail Order Business Directory
Lists over 10,000 mail order and
catalog houses

•**From Oxbridge
Communications, Inc.**
150 Fifth Avenue
New York, NY 10011
212-741-0231

College Media Directory

Oxbridge Directory of Newsletters

•**Books from publishers with
one reference**

Book Buyers Handbook
American Booksellers Association
560 White Plains Road
Tarrytown, NY 10591
Fax: 914-631-8391

Broadcasting/Cable Yearbook
1705 DeSales Street, NW
Washington, DC 20036

***Dewey Decimal Classification
and Relative Index***

Forest Press, Inc.
85 Watervliet Avenue
Albany, NY 12206-2082
518-489-8549

Direct Mail List Rate & Data
Standard Rate and Data Service, Inc.
3004 Glenview Road
Wilmette, IL 60091
708-256-6067

***Directory of Specialized
American Bookdealers***
The Moretus Press
P.O. Box 1080
Ossining, NY 10562-1080

***Directory of Specialized
Bookdealers in the U.K. Handling
Mainly New Books***
Peter Marcan Publications
31, Rowliff Road
High Wycombe, Bucks., HP12 3LD
Great Britain

Larimi Media Guides
5 W. 37th St., New York, NY 10018

***Membership Directory
Marketing to Libraries through
Library Associations***
American Library Association
50 East Huron Street
Chicago, IL 60611-2795

National Union Catalog
Library of Congress
Available in your local library

***The* (British) *Post Office Direct
Mail Handbook***
Les Andrews, Exley Publications
16 Chalk Hill
Watford, Herts WD1 4BN
Great Britain

*Proofreading Manual and
Reference Guide
Directory of Editorial
Resources*
Editorial Experts
66 Canal Center Plaza, Suite 200
Alexandria, VA 22314
703-683-0683

*Self-Publish Your Own Picture
Book*
Howard Gregory
640 The Village #209
Redondo Beach, CA 9027

Talk Show Guest Directory
Mitchell P. Davis
2233 Wisconsin Avenue NW #406-P
Washington, DC 20007-4104

Working Press of the Nation
Reed Reference Publishing
Bryan Newman
R.R. Bowker Catalog
121 Chanlon Road
New Providence, NJ 07974
908-464-6800/800-521-8110
Lists newspapers, magazines,
radio, TV, feature writers and
internal publications

American Publishers Directory

International Books in Print

*International Directory of
Booksellers*

*Publishers International
Directory*

World Guide to Libraries

•**From Writer's Digest Books**
1507 Dana Avenue
Cincinnati, OH 45207

Writer's Market

Writer's Yearbook

Writer's Digest Books also publishes many specific publishing
books such as how to publish
cookbooks, children's books, etc.

USEFUL STUFF, Part 3
Magazines for Publishers

ALA Booklist
50 East Huron Street
Chicago, IL 60611
312-944-6780

American Bookseller Magazine
560 White Plains Road
Tarrytown, NY 10591
914-631-7800

Canadian Author & Bookman
P.O. Box 120
Niagara-On-The-Lake, ON L0S 1J0
Canada

Choice
Patricia E. Sabosik
100 Riverview Center
Middletown, CT 06457
203-347-6933

Horn Book Magazine
Anita Silvey
14 Beacon St.
Boston, MA 02108
800-325-1170/617-227-1555
Children's Books

Kirkus Reviews
Anne Larsen
200 Park Avenue South
New York, NY 10003

Library Journal
249 West 17th Street
New York, NY 10011
212-645-0067

**Publishers Marketing
Association Newsletter**
Jan Nathan
2401 Pacific Coast Hwy #102
Hermosa Beach, CA 90254
310-372-2732

Publishers Weekly
249 West 17th Street
New York, NY 10011
212-645-0067

School Library Journal
249 West 17th Street
New York, NY 10011
212-645-0067

Direct Response Specialist
Galen Stilson
P.O. Box 1075
Tarpon Spring, FL 34688

Publishing Poynters (free)
Dan Poynter
P.O. Box 4232
Santa Barbara, CA 93140-4232
FAX-ON-DEMAND 805-968-8947

Sharing Ideas
Royal Publishing, Inc.
Dottie Walters
P.O. Box 1120
Glendora, CA 91740
818-335-8069
Cassettes, books, speakers agency,
speakers seminars

Signature
Griffin Printing
Rick Ford
544 West Colorado Street
Glendale, CA 91204-1102
800-826-4849 (US)

USEFUL STUFF, Part 4
Newsletters

Best-Seller Books
Ernest Weckbaugh, Editor
1718 Rogers Place, #1A
Burbank, CA 91504
818-842-4278
Techniques from successful book
promoters

Book Marketing Update
John Kremer
P.O. Box 1102
Fairfield, IA 52556
515-472-6130

USEFUL STUFF, Part 5 ...
Pamphlet and Reports

Chicago Advertising Agency
28 East Jackson Boulevard
Chicago, IL 60604

Ad Guide
(Circulation and ad prices for
numerous magazines)

**Copyright Office, Library of
Congress**
Washington, DC 20559

Circular 1, **Copyright Basics**

Circular 2, *Publications on Copyright*

Federal Trade Commission
Washington, DC 20580

Consumer Alert —
The Vanity Press
(News release dated 7/19/1959)

FTC Buyer's Guide No. 2

Shopping By Mail?
You're Protected!

Vanity Press Findings
(Docket 7005 and 7489)

P.E.N. American Center
568 Broadway
New York, NY 10012

Grants and Awards Available
to American Writers

National Endowment for the
Arts, Literature Program
Nancy Hanks Center
1100 Pennsylvania Ave., NW
Washington, DC 20506-0001

Assistance, fellowships
and residences for writers

Poets & Writers
72 Spring Street
New York, NY 10012

Awards List

Literary Bookstores in the U.S.

Sponsors List

Writer's Guide to Copyright

Popular Mechanics Classified
224 West 57th Street
New York, NY 10019

Profits from Classified Ads

Small Business Administration
409 3rd Street
Washington, DC 20416
202-205-6600/800-827-5722

Directory of Business Develop-
ment Publications
General business guidance and
booklets for the new publisher.
Send for a list of available publications covering many subjects.

USEFUL STUFF, Part 6
Delivery by Mail

Express Mail Service
Handbook DM201
U.S. Postal Service
Eastern Area Supply Center
Somerville, NJ 08877-0001.
Policies, regulations and proce-
dures for Express Mail Service.
$1.00 subscription

Domestic Mail Manual
Superintendent of Documents
U.S. Government Printing Office
Washington, DC 20402-0001
202-783-3238
Complete rules, regulations and
postal rate information for all
classes of mail sent and received in
the U.S. $17.00 for four revisions,
issued as needed.

International Mail Manual
Superintendent of Documents
U.S. Government Printing Office
Washington, DC 20402-0001
202-783-3238
Complete rules, procedures,
regulations and postal rate
information for all classes of mail
sent out of the U.S. $14.00 per
looseleaf edition, issued as needed

*National Five-Digit ZIP Code
and Post Office Directory
(Publication 65A)*
U.S. Postal Service—800-238-3150
Order Form 4243. Call for prices

Postal Bulletin
Superintendent of Documents
U.S. Government Printing Office
Washington, DC 20402-0001
Weekly newsletter providing specific
details on procedures, rates and
regulations. $71.00 per year

ZIP+4 State Directory
U.S. Postal Service—800-238-3150
Order Form 4242. Call for prices

The following publications are
available free from your local Post
Office. Many deal with direct
mail (bulk rate, pre-sort, etc.)
rather than parcel post, but as
long as you are collecting information at the Post Office, you
might as well get everything.

Addressing for Automation
Notice 221

*Bar Code/FIM Pattern Locater
Gauge*
Model 005

Basic Addressing
Notice 23A

*A Bottom Line Estimate of Your
Presort Savings*
Notice 243

*Computer Programming for
Presort First-Class Mail*
Notice 244

*Directory of ZIP+4 Coding
Services*
Publication 148

*Express Mail International
Services Guide*
Publication 273

Express Mail Rate Charts
Poster 189

*A Guide to Business Mail
Preparation*
Publication 25

*How to Prepare Presort
First-Class Mail*
Poster 89

*Information Guide on Presort
First Class Mail*
Publication 61

International Postal Rates &Fees
Publication 51

*International Priority Airmail
Mailer Guidelines*
Publication 507

*International Surface Airlift,
(ISAL) Service Guide*
Notice 82A

*INTERPOST Service Director
and Users Guide*
Notice 82A

Mailer's Guide
Publication 19

Metered Better, Treated Better
Notice 125

National Change of Address
Notice 47

On-site Meter Setting
Notice 112

*Postal Rates, Fees and
Information*
Notice 59

*Preparing Business and
Courtesy Reply Mail*
Publication 12

*ZIP+4 Codes...Why They Add
Up for Business Mailers*
Notice 186

*ZIP+4: Helping You Help Your
Business*
Notice 189

USEFUL STUFF, Part 7
Selling to the Government

U.S. Information Service
Attn: Resource Development Br.
301 Fourth Street SW #314 (E/CLD)
Washington, DC 20547

**Send for the following
government publications to:**

Superintendent of Documents
U.S. Government Printing Office
Washington, DC 20402
202-783-3238

*Doing Business with the Federal
Government*
#022-003-01136-6 $2.50

Selling to the Government $1.50

Selling to the Military
#008-000-479-0 $8.00

*Starting and Managing a
Business from Your Home*
Vol. 102 $2.00

*Starting and Managing
a Small Business
of Your Own*
Vol.1 045-000-00212-8 $4.75

*U.S. Government Purchasing
and Sales Directory* $5.50

USEFUL STUFF, Part 8
In The Dumps!

Many non-bookstore accounts will
require a "dump" to properly display your books. Bookstores have
bookshelves but most other stores
do not. A dump is a counter or floor
display made of corrugated card-
board. It is filled with books and
usually comes in its own corrugated
carton shipper.

Ironwood Displays
P.O. Box 632
Niles, MI 49120
616-683-8500

Loizeaux Brothers
Peter Bartlett, President
1238 Corlies Avenue
Neptune, NJ 07754
908-922-6665/800-526-2796

Mercury Die and Container
3201 West Mission Road
Alhambra, CA 91803
213-685-7565

Midwest Fiber Products
P.O. Box 397
Viola, IL 61486
309-596-2955

Screen Art Posters
4333 East 10th Lane
Hialeah, FL 33013
305-681-4641

OFF THE SHELF ...
Fulfillment Houses

Central Distribution Services
Steve Rudminas
8361 U.S. Highway 45
Neenah, WI 54956
414-722-2848

JV Company
Ben Rose, CEO
P.O. Box 11950
Reno, NV 89510
702-359-9811

Matrixx Marketing
Bret Butterfiald
4931 South 900 East
Salt Lake City, UT 84117
800-654-8000/800-265-3000
Telemarketing Company

Professional Book Distributors
Michael W. Linville
2727 Scioto Parkway
Columbia, OH 43220
Fax 614-771-1875

Publishers Fulfillment Group/
Educational Clearing House
4721 Capital Circle SW
Tallahassee, FL 32310
904-878-0522
Educational clearing house

Publishers Storage & Shipping
Peter Quick, V.P.
660 S. Mansfield
Ypsilanti, MI 48197
313-487-9720

Publishers Storage & Shipping
E.B. Quick
46 Development Road
Fitchburg, MA 01420
508-435-2121

St. Joe Distributing
Joel Savino, President
Brooklyn Navy Yard, #3
Brooklyn, NY 11205
718-834-0170

Team Distribution Center
Herbert Roundtree, P.O. Box 2248
Wayne, NJ 07474-2248
201-595-1751

Upper Access Books
P.O. Box 457
One Upper Access Road
Hinesburg, VT 05461
800-356-9315

HORIZONS, Part 1
Wholesalers (W) / Distributors (D)

Academic Book Center (W)
5600 NE Hassalo Street
Portland, OR 97213
503-287-6657/800-547-7704
Fax 503-284-8859

Advanced Marketing Svs (W)
5880 Oberlin Drive #400
San Diego, CA 92121-9653
619-457-2500

Ambassador Book Service (W)
42 Chasner Street
Hempstead, NY 11550
516-489-4011

Atrium Publishing Group (D)
11270 Clayton Creek Road
Lowerlake, CA 95467
707-995-3906/800-275-2606
Fax 707-995-1814

Baker & Taylor Co., Publ. (W)
Contact Section
652 East Main Street
P.O. Box 6920
Bridgewater, NJ 08807-0920
908-218-3969/Fax 908-218-3980

Ballen Booksellers Intl. (W)
125 Ricefield Lane
Hauppauge, NY 11788
516-543-5600/Fax 516-864-5850

Blackwell North American (W)
100 Fries Mill Road
Blackwood, NJ 08012
609-629-0700/Fax 609-629-0438

Blackwell North American (W)
6024 SW Jean Road, Bldg. G
Lake Oswego, OR 97035
503-684-1140/Fax 503-639-2481

Bookazine Co. (W)
Fran Stone
75 Hook Road
Bayonne, NJ 07002
201-339-7777/Fax: 201-339-7778

Book House, Inc. (W)
208 West Chicago Street
Jonesville, MI 49250-0125
517-849-2117/Fax 517-849-9716

The Bookmen, Inc. (W)
John Kudrle, Buyer
525 North Third Street
Minneapolis, MN 55401-1296
612-341-3333/Fax: 612-341-2903
800-328-8411 or 800-622-3584 (MN)

Book Dynamics (W)
5/800-441-4510
26 Kenney Blvd.
East Brunswick, NJ 08816
908-545-5151/800-441-4510
Fax: 908-862-1639

The Booksource (W)
Sandy Jaffe, Owner
4127 Forest Park
St. Louis, MO 63108
314-652-1000/800-444-0435
Fax: 314-652-1635

Bookpeople (W)
7900 Edgewater Drive
Oakland, CA 94710
510-632-470/800-999-4650
Fax 510-632-1281

Brodart Company (W)
500 Arch Street
Williamsport, PA 17705
717-326-2461/800-233-8467
Fax 717-326-6769

Cannon Book Distribution (D)
25 Connell Court, #2
Toronto, ON M8Z 1E8
Canada
416-252-5207/Fax: 416-253-9445

The Distributors (W)
702 South Michigan
South Bend, IN 46618
219-232-8500/800-348-5200

Golden-Lee Book Distributors (W)
1000 Dean Street
Brooklyn, NY 11238
718-857-6333/800-221-0960
Fax 718-857-5997

Inland Book Company (W)
P.O. Box 120470
East Haven, CT 06512
203-467-4257/800-243-0138
Fax 203-469-7697

Ingram Book Company (W)
One Ingram Blvd.
Lavergne, TN 37086-1986
615-793-5000/Fax 615-793-3825

International Service Company (W)
333 Fourth Avenue
Indialantic, FL 32903
305-724-1443

Koen Book Distributors (W)
10 Twosome Dr.
Moorestown, NJ 08057
609-235-4444/800-257-8481
Fax 609-235-6914

L-S Distributors (W)
Bob Belmont, Book Buyer
130 East Grand Avenue
South San Francisco, CA 94080
415-873-2094/800-654-7040
Fax: 415-873-4222

Merle Distributing (W)
27222 Plymouth Road
Detroit, MI 48239-2395
313-937-8400/800-233-9380
Fax: 313-937-8380

Midwest Library Service (W)
11443 Charles Rock Road
Bridgeton, MO 63044-2789
314-739-3100

Moving Books, Inc. (W)
P.O. Box 20037
Seattle, WA 98102
206-762-1705/800-777-6683
Fax: 206-762-1896

New England Mobile Book Fair (W)
82 Needham Street
Newton Highlands, MA 02161
617-527-5817/617527-0113
800-225-4264

New Leaf Distributing (W)
5425 Tulane Dr. SW
Atlanta, GA 30336-2323
404-691-6996/Fax 800-326-1066

Pacific Pipeline (W)
8030 S. 228th
Kent, WA 98032-1171
206-872-5523/Fax 206-872-0849

Publishers Distribution Service (D)
6893 Sullivan Road
Grawn, MI 49637
616-276-5196/800-345-0096
Fax 276-5197/800-507-BOOK

Publishers Group West (D)
4065 Hollis Street
Emeryville, CA 94662
510-658-3453/800-788-3123
Fax 510-658-1834

Quality Books (D)
918 Sherwood Drive
Lake Bluff, IL 60044-2204
708-295-2010/Fax: 708-295-1556

Unique Books
4230 Grove Avenue
Gurnee, IL 60031
708-623-9171/800-553-5446
/Fax 708-623-7238

SCB Distributors (D)
15612 New Century Drive
Gardena, CA 90248
310-532-9400/Fax: 310-532-7001

Southern Book Service (W)
Palmetto Lakes Industrial Park
5154 NW 165 Street
Hialeah, FL 33014-6335
305-624-4545/800-843-6568
Fax 305-621-0425

Sunbelt Publications (W)
8630 Argent, #C
Santee, CA 92071
619-258-4911/800-626-6579
Fax: 619-258-4916
Nature, recreation, travel and
regional books

HORIZONS, Part 2
Directories of Bookstores

Barnes & Noble Bookstores
105 Fifth Avenue
New York, NY 10003
212-633-3300

Coles Bookstores
90 Ronson Drive
Etobicoke M9W, ON 1C1 Canada
416-243-3132/Fax 416-243-8964

Crown Books
3300 75th Avenue
Landover, MD 20785
301-731-1200/Fax 301-773-2705

Doubleday Bookshops
724 Fifth Avenue
New York, NY 10019
212-397-0550

**Little Professor
Book Centers**
John Glazer, President
130 South First Street #300
Ann Arbor, MI 48104
313-994-1212/Fax 313-944-9009

W.H. Smith Ltd.
Buying Manager
113 Merton Street
Toronto, ON M4S 1A8
Canada
416-485-6660/Fax 416-485-2161

HORIZONS, Part 3
Mailing List Brokers

Advanced Publishing Systems
403 Grand Central Avenue
Lavallette, NJ 08735
908-793-5600
College professors

American Business Lists
P.O. Box 27347
Omaha, NE 68127
402-331-7169
14 million businesses compiled from
Yellow Pages.

American Direct Marketing Svs
1120 Empire Central Pl., Ste. 320
Dallas, TX 75247
214-688-1911/800-527-5080
Compiler

American Library Assn.
50 East Huron Street

Chicago, IL 60611
312-944-6780
Libraries

American List Council
88 Orchard Road-CN 5219
Princeton, NJ 08543
904-874-4300/800-526-3973
Book buyers

R.R. Bowker Lists
John Panza
245 West 17th Street
New York, NY 10011
Publishing industry

Ed Burnett Consultants
99 West Sheffield Avenue
Englewood, NJ 07631
201-871-1100/800-223-7777
General

Compilers Plus
466 Main Street
New Rochelle, NY 10801
914-738-1520/914-633-5240
800-431-2914

Consolidated Mailing Service
Max Bradbard
P.O. Box 495
St. James, NY 11780
516-584-7283
Academic

Dunhill International
2430 West Oakland Park Blvd.
Ft. Lauderdale, FL 33311
Executives

Dustbooks
Len Fulton
P.O. Box 100
Paradise, CA 95969

Executive Services Company
Response+
901 North International Parkway
Richardson, TX 75081
214-699-1271/800-527-3933
Buyers by age

Fleetwood Communications
H.A. Bezanson
P.O. Box 2134
Blaine, WA 98231
604-278-2560
Canadian schools, libraries, hospitals and newspapers

Hugo Dunhill Lists
630 Third Avenue
New York, NY 10017
212-682-8030/800-223-6454
General

IBIS Information Services
152 Madison Avenue
New York, NY 10016
212-779-1344/800-433-6226
Foreign

Mailings Clearing House
601 East Marshall Street
Sweet Springs, MO 65351
816-335-6373
Academic

Market Data Retrieval
16 Progress Drive
Shelton, CT 06484
800-243-5538/800-435-3742 (CT)
Libraries and schools

ParaLists
P.O. Box 4232
Santa Barbara, CA 93140-4232
805-968-7277
FAX-ON-DEMAND 805-968-8947

PCS Mailing Lists
85 Constitution Lane
Danvers, MA 01923
617-532-1600/800-532-5478
Compiler/broker

Quality Education Data
1600 Broadway, 12th Floor
Denver, CO 80202
800-525-5811
Schools

R.L. Polk & Company
6400 Monroe Blvd.
Taylor, MI 48180
313-292-3200
General

Edith Roman Lists
253 West 35th Street, 16th Floor
New York, NY 10001
212-695-3836/800-223-2194
Compiler/broker

Southam Direct Marketing
12 Nantucket Blvd.
Scarborough, ON M1P 4W7 Canada
Canadian schools, libraries,
bookstores, doctors and businesses

SpeciaLISTS
1200 Harbor Blvd., 9th Floor
Weehawken, NJ 07087
201-865-5800

Wilson Marketing Group
11924 Washington Blvd.
Los Angeles, CA 90066
310-398-2754
Institutional

Fred Woolf Lists
110 Corporate Park Drive
White Plains, NY 10604
914-694-4466
800-431-1557
Compiler/broker

Stevens-Knox & Assoc.
304 Park Ave., South, 6th Floor
New York, NY 10010
212-685-4600/212-388-8800
Book buyers

Worldata
P.O. Box 443
Jericho, NY 11753
(516) 931-2442
General

Alvin B. Zeller, Inc.
224 Fifth Ave., New York, NY 10001
212-689-4900/800-223-0814

Zeller & Letica
15 East 26th Street
New York, NY 10010
212-685-7512/800-221-4112

Also see *The Encyclopedia of Associations* and other references. Most organizations rent their mailing lists.

HORIZONS, Part 4
I Wanna Be In Pictures!

Book Publicists—These professionals will schedule you for TV appearances, write your news releases and introduce you to other media contacts. For an expanded listing, see *Literary Market Place*.

Frank Promotion Company
Ben G. Frank
60 East 42nd Street #2119
New York, NY 10017
212-687-3383

Gaughen Public Relations
Barbara Gaughen
226 East Canon Perdido, #B1
Santa Barbara, CA 93101
805-965-8482/Fax: 805-965-6522
FAX-ON-DEMAND: 805-96-FAX-IT
Book publicity seminars and
public appearance management

The Marketing Source
Ruth Klein
5330 Office Center Ct.
Bakersfield, CA 93309
805-324-4687/Fax: 325-0520
Preparation of sales presentations,
business feature writing, book tours

Planned Television Arts
Rick Frishman
25 West 43rd Street
New York, NY 10036

Promotion in Motion
Irwin Zucker
6464 Sunset Blvd., #580
Hollywood, CA 90028-8007
213-461-3921/Fax: 213-461-0917
Book publicity

Radio/TV Interview Report
Bradley Communications
135 East Plumstead Avenue
Lansdowne, PA 19050
800-989-1400
Fax: 215-284-3704
Provides talk show guests and ideas
to radio & television producers

Wireless Flash
Wireless Flash Company
Patrick Glynn
Nikki Godfrey
405 W. Washington St., #224
San Diego, CA 92103
(619) 543-8940

Instant daily communication of book
related news items to radio stations
nationwide

HORIZONS, Part 5
Book Fairs

Conference Book Service
80 South Early Street
Alexandria, VA 22314

COSMEP Exhibit Service
P.O. Box 420703
San Francisco, CA 94142-0703
415-922-9490/Fax: 415-922-5566

Independent Publishers Services.
P.O. Box 135
Volcano, CA 95689
209-296-7989

PMA Book Exhibits
2401 Pacific Coast Highway #109-A
Hermosa Beach, CA 90254

HORIZONS, Part 6
Letting the Catalog Out of
the Bookbag

The Catalog of Catalogs
Woodbine House
5615 Fishers Lane
Rockville, MD 20852
301-468-8800/800-843-7323

Catalog Handbook
Enterprise Magazines
1020 North Broadway, #111-P
Milwaukee, WI 53202
414-272-9977/Fax: 414-272-9973
Lists over 5,000 catalogs by product
category, $6.95 postpaid

Directory of Mail Order Catalogs
Grey House Publishing
P.O. Box 1866
Pocket Knife Square
Lakeville, CT 06069
203-435-0868/Fax: 203-435-0867
800-562-2139
Lists 6,300 mail order catalogs

Great Catalog Guide
Direct Marketing Association
6 East 43rd Street
New York, NY 10017
212-768-7277

**The International Catalogue
of Catalogues**
Harper-Collins
10 East 53rd Street
New York, NY 10022
212-207-7000

The Kid's Catalog Collection
Globe Pequot Press
6 Business Park Rd., P.O. Box 833,
Old Saybrook, CT 06475-0833
203-395-0440
Over 500 catalogs that feature books,
toys, clothing, etc., for children

Mail Order Business Directory
B. Klein Publications
P.O. Box 8503
Coral Springs, FL 33075
305-752-1708/Fax: 305-752-2547

National Directory of Catalogs
Oxbridge Communications
150 Fifth Avenue #636
New York, NY 10011-4311
212-741-0231/Fax: 212- 633-2938
Lists 7,000 U.S. and Canadian
catalogs, 457 that carry books

**Marketing Forum
Wholesalers Buying Guide**
Wilshire Book Company
12015-A Sherman Road
North Hollywood, CA 91605
818-765-8579

Wholesale by Mail Catalog
by The Print Project
St. Martins Press, 175 Fifth Ave.
New York, NY 10010
212-674-5151

Magazines for the catalog business
are listed below. Some list your book
and offer it to catalogs. Send for
samples and prices.

Catalog Age/Catalog Product News
P.O. Box 4949
Stamford, CT 06907-0949
203-358-9900/Fax: 203-357-9014
800-775-3777

The best book on the subject is an
unassuming but jam-packed 50-pager
titled *Selling to Catalog Houses* by Ron
Playle, Send $10.95 to:

Para Publishing
Dan Poynter, P.O. Box 4232
Santa Barbara, CA 93140-4232
805-968-7277/Fax: 805-968-1379
FAX-ON-DEMAND 805-968-8947

MAJOR CATALOGS

Hanover House Industries
1500 Harbor Blvd.
Weehawken, NJ 07087
201-863-7300/Fax: 201-319-3478

Harriet Carter
425 Stump Road
Montgomeryville, PA 18936
215-361-5122

Publisher's Clearinghouse
Jeannie Clark
382 Channel Drive
Port Washington, NY 11050
516-883-5432/Fax: 516-767-3650

HORIZONS, Part 7
Help! Special Technical and Media Services

Casa Graphics, Inc.
Ernest Weckbaugh (author/designer)
1718 Rogers Place #1A
Burbank, CA 91504
818-842-4278/Fax: 818-842-2960
Nearly 50 years of experience in graphics (specializing in cover design, photography, typesetting, book design and illustration) and writing (contract author with two major publishing houses, ghost writer, editor and public relations feature writer).

Gaughen Fishing
(Pronounced "Gone")
Gaughen Public Relations
226 East Canon Perdido, Suite B
Santa Barbara, CA 93101
(805) 965-8482/Fax: (805) 965-6522
A monthly publication to 250 of the nation's key radio and TV talk show producers. Positions you as an expert spokesperson with timely news angles and clever feature ideas...*the hooks for reeling in big audiences!*

Wordwise
P.O. Box 525
Citrus Heights, CA 95611-0525
916-649-2440/916-726-1384
Professional writing and editing service for manuscripts.

BARBARA GAUGHEN, a highly successful practitioner of the "New PR," has been the inspiration and motivation for hundreds of businesses, governmental agencies, authors and professionals in promoting their products and services.

A socially responsible agency, Gaughen Public Relations is a four-time winner of *Business Digest's* "Best of Business Award" in the public relations category. In 1990, Gaughen was voted "Business Person of the Year." She brings her unique public relations approach to local, national and international clientele. Her personal mentor is none other than Edward L. Bernays, considered the "Father of Public Relations."

A dynamic and informational speaker and writer, Barbara has appeared on over three hundred radio and thirty television talk shows. She has written *Getting the World to Beat a Path to Your Door* and hundreds of articles for trade journals. Drawing on over twenty years of public relations counseling, she has developed a specialty in book promotion. Her book publicity workshops are offered nationwide.

Teaming with a local television station, she co-produced a series of book workshops entitled *The Book Publicity and Public Relations Seminar* that ran for five years. Due to overwhelming response, the material and ideas from these workshops were collected into the *60 Steps for "Instant" Book Success* that became the basis for this book.

Gaughen holds a BA in Education from San Diego State University and has completed her masters requirements in leadership and research design from University of California, Santa Barbara and San Diego State University.

Gaughen Public Relations is headquartered in Santa Barbara, California, with branch offices in Ventura, Burbank and Hollywood.

ERNEST WECKBAUGH began his working life at the age of five as a child actor under contract to Warner Bros. Studios. Among twenty or more films, he appeared in a half-dozen of the later episodes of the *Our Gang Comedies.*

His career as a graphic artist and writer started with a tour of duty in the United States Air Force in Alaska where he served as a member of Special Services as a performer and an artist/ illustrator in the entertainment unit.

He graduated with high honors from California State University at Los Angeles with a bachelors degree in fine arts, and has lectured at UCLA and USC on small business marketing and on brochure writing. He has conducted art classes for the Glendale (California) City School District and for the Walt Disney Studios in Burbank.

He is a professional speaker and MC, a Past President of his Toastmasters club and he has been elected Toastmaster of the Year seven times.

President of Casa Graphics, Inc. of Burbank, CA, since 1976, he added newspaper journalism to his creative skills in 1985, authoring a weekly feature column for the Leader Newspapers in the San Gabriel Valley for a number of years and, later, for the Los Angeles Daily News. He has been involved in creating a series of nonfiction books on a variety of subjects either as author, co-author, ghostwriter, editor or illustrator.

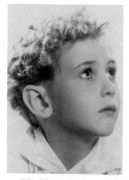

Weckbaugh at age six
(Warner Bros. contract player)

Appendix I

GAUGHEN PUBLIC RELATIONS
PR & Book Publicity Questionnaire

Title of Book: _____

Publication Date: _____

Author: _____

Phone (day): (____)_____ Fax: (____)_____(800)_____

Person filling out questionnaire:_____

Phone (day): (____)_____ Fax: (____)_____

Relationship to the book: _____

1. DEFINE SUCCESS
What do you want to happen as a result of the PR and publicity campaign?

_____

_____

_____

_____

_____

_____

_____

_____

_____

_____

_____

_____

_____

2. WHERE ARE YOU NOW?

A. What stage of writing your book have you reached?

❏ Concept
❏ Still writing
❏ Complete manuscript
❏ Off the press
❏ In the bookstores

B. Your distributor (name)_____

C. Your wholesaler (name)_____

D. How many books have you . . .

❏ written? _____

❏ self-published?_____

❏ had published?_____

3. PROMOTION

A. If you have already published or had a book(s) published, describe a past book promotion success.

_____

_____

_____

_____

_____

_____

_____

_____

_____

_____

_____

B. Are you planning to handle the promotion for your current book? ❏ Yes ❏ No

4. PLAN

If the answer to #3B is yes:

A. Do you have a plan? ❏ Yes ❏ No

B. What is your PR budget?_____

C. How much time do you plan to spend promoting your book every week?_____hours

D. Describe any PR efforts you may have already completed for your current book.

_____

_____

_____

_____

_____

_____

_____

_____

_____

_____

_____

_____

_____

_____

_____

_____

_____

_____

_____

_____

5. MEDIA SPOKESPERSON

Who will be the spokesperson/media star for your book?

A. Describe the benefits and background of this person.

B. How much experience have they had with the media, keynote speaking, seminars, speeches? Please describe . . .

_____

_____

_____

_____

_____

_____

_____

_____

_____

_____

_____

_____

_____

_____

_____

_____

_____

_____

_____

_____

C. Check off the following areas of past experience for your spokesperson:

❑ Face to face interviews ❑ Newspaper articles by author ❑ Speaker

❑ Phone interviews ❑ Newspaper interviews ❑ Author tour

❑ Radio talk shows by phone ❑ Television talk shows ❑ Book signings

❑ Radio talk shows in person ❑ TV features, ads, infomercials ❑ Others, please list:

❑ Magazine interviews ❑ Television news

_____

_____

6. A PROMOTION IDEA

A. What is the most outrageous, bizarre or unusual promotion idea you've come up with for this book?

_____

_____

_____

_____

_____

_____

_____

_____

_____

_____

B. How could it work?

_____

_____

_____

_____

_____

_____

_____

_____

_____

_____

_____

_____

Glossary

Advertising Promotion you pay for.

Angle A style of writing used in a news release that gives it a powerful appeal when read by editors and their readers, listeners or viewers.

Bestseller When quality writing, good production values and an outstanding publicity effort combine to create sales for a book that cause a demand for multiple printings and bring in a substantial return on the publisher's investment.

Bio Biographic information about the author included in the news release.

Book clubs Direct-mail, book-selling organizations such as the Book-of-the-Month Club (Time, Inc.) and Literary Guild (Doubleday Book Clubs).

Book fairs A locally-organized open market for books, usually put on as a fund-raiser for the arts or other worthy causes.

Bound galleys A manuscript printout or a sampling of an opening chapter or two (with an annotated table of contents) to indicate to an editor or reviewer what the book is about and the quality of your writing.

Bounce-back A business-reply post card order form designed to make it easy for decision-makers to respond as soon as they receive your press kit.

Brochure Sales-promotion literature, listing the unique features of a book, a product or a service, often printed on six panels of an 8-1/2 x 11-inch sheet folded to fit a #10 envelope.

Byline The name of the author printed over a published

newspaper or magazine article or story.

Column A regularly-published article under the byline of a staff or freelance writer.

Condensation rights Allowing a magazine to publish a condensed version (all or several chapters) as an article or series of articles.

Co-op advertising When a publisher and bookseller share the cost of promoting a sale or an autograph-signing party.

Copy Written information—articles, stories, advertisements, news releases, etc.

Clip file (Clips) A collection of published or broadcast articles, stories or publicity releases.

Clip reel Videotaped copies of past interviews or appearances.

Cover letter (Pitch letter) A one-page letter that summarizes the materials to which it is attached, giving background information and emphasizing areas of media interest.

Cutline Also called a caption, it is the attached information that identifies the people or objects in a photograph or in a piece of artwork.

Deadline The scheduled time at which a supplier (writer, photographer, printer, etc.) is required to submit the completed project for publication or broadcast.

Double-spaced Setting of the lines in a manuscript with a blank space between each line.

Editor A person, either working on the media staff or freelance, who controls the writing quality of submitted articles or stories.

Fact sheet An information list sent to the media about a person, an organization, a service or a product.

Fax (facsimile) An electronic means of transmitting either printed or handwritten information, graphic or photographic images.

Flyer Like a brochure, but usually printed on one side of an 8-1/2 x 11-inch sheet in letter-format.

Glossy A photograph with a shiny surface (usually black and white).

Halftone A photograph, which is screened into a pattern of small dots in order to be printed on a press.

Independent bookstore Generally a small, locally-owned store, as contrasted with a large, centrally-administered, chain-store type of operation

Lead The first paragraph of an article, story or advertising piece written to arouse interest.

Live The airing of an interview or program on radio or television as it occurs (not recorded).

Marketing A publisher's total plan for selling a book, including display advertising, reviews, media releases, premiums, public appearance tours by the author, periodical and subsidiary rights, book fairs, and the contacting of book clubs, libraries, non-traditional retailers, the ABA, wholesalers, distributors, etc.

Media kit A collection of essential information in a folder— cover letter, fact sheets, photographs, biography, artwork, copies of published articles, reviews, financial information, etc.

News (press) conference An event staged for the benefit of the media so that they may conveniently hear an important announcement regarding a new book, product or service, etc.

News release Sheet containing newsworthy information about a person, book, product, service, etc., to be delivered or mailed to the various media (also called a **press release**, if sent only to the print media).

Non-traditional markets Retailers other than bookstores (gift stores, grocery stores, hobby shops, etc.) or tradeshows, gatherings, conventions, reunions, etc., that draw an audience interested in your subject.

Periodical rights Allowing a magazine to publish an excerpt (a chapter or part of a chapter) from your book as an article or series of articles.

Premium An arrangement made with a manufacturer whose sales of a related product(s) would benefit from the public reading your book. Discount coupons in your book for their product, or ads on their products' packages offering a discount on your book, help both parties.

Pre-publication ad A carefully-placed display advertisement announcing to your target audience your book will be available soon, for the purpose of generating advanced orders.

Publicity A form of promotion that is printed or broadcast free of charge, because it is timely or newsworthy.

Public relations The total effort involved in creating a positive image on behalf of a person, product, service, business, organization, charity, etc.

Public Service Announcement (PSA) An announcement submitted to the media for an event of public interest that is free or of minimal cost.

Query letter A brief summary of your book idea, including who you are (short bio) and what you've written (attach list of credits and clips). Send to a list of selected editors who are most likely to deal with your kind of subject.

Release date The date a news item needs to appear in print or on the air.

Review A short magazine article about your book that informs and encourages the decision-makers in bookstores and libraries to place orders with your distributor.

Review copies Complimentary books sent to magazines or newsletters by the author, publisher or publicist.

Special edition An upcoming issue of a publication with a theme or focused on an issue that relates to your book's subject in which you might place a "promotional" article.

Specialty (or specialized) bookstores Retailers who handle only one kind of subject (mystery, children, aviation, etc.).

Stat sheet A fact sheet that contains primarily numerical or statistical data.

Strategic plan A business plan for the most effective marketing of your book to your target audience.

Target audience The group(s) of people who are most likely to be interested in your book's subject, and probably account for most of its sales.

Targeted organizations Large groups whose members share a common interest in the subject of your book. Contact them to arrange speeches, fund-raising sales, annual convention booth space, endorsements, testimonials, etc.

30 (xxx) A commonly used symbol that indicates the end of a news release or editorial.

Trade publication A magazine or newsletter distributed only to a specific industry.

Wire Service An agency whose purpose is to compile and supply news to the national and international media.

Index